THE NOBLE SAVAGES

Bryan R. Wilson

The Noble Savages

The Primitive Origins of Charisma

and Its Contemporary Survival

University of California Press

Berkeley · Los Angeles · London

University of California Press
Berkeley and Los Angeles, California

University of California Press, Ltd.
London, England

Copyright © 1975, by
The Regents of the University of California

ISBN 0-520-02815-5
Library of Congress Catalog Card Number: 74-81444
Printed in the United States of America

Contents

Now we begin to understand the old motto, Noblesse Oblige. Noblesse means having the gift of power, the natural or sacred power. And having such power obliges a man to act with fearlessness and generosity, responsible for his acts to God. A noble is one who may be known before all men.

Some men must be noble, or life is an ash-heap. There is natural nobility, given by God or the Unknown, and far beyond common sense. And towards natural nobility we must live. The simple man, whose best self, his noble self, is nearly all the time puzzled, dumb, and helpless, has still the power to recognize the man in whom the noble self is powerful and articulate. To this man he must pledge himself.

D. H. LAWRENCE
"Epilogue" in *Movements in European History*
London: O.U.P. Original Edn 1921
(published with the original
"Epilogue" first in 1971)

Preface

In examining charismatic leadership in primitive societies, this essay seeks to explore simultaneously a number of related themes. Weber gave relatively little attention to primitive cultures, although the belief that a charismatic leader would arise may have become a tradition, and may indeed have had its origins, among just such peoples. In these societies, the charismatic claimant is, of necessity, a claimant to essentially supernatural power, for within these cultures everything is conceived in at least partially magico-religious terms: thus, even leaders who do not themselves assume a religious role claim supernatural power, whether magical or mystical. The only claim that could hope to stand against constituted authority among these, and indeed among more-developed peoples, was a claim to power from a transcendent source, great enough to be set over against existing power structures (which themselves usually rested on supernatural legitimations). It is thus in the stronger sense of divinely inspired power that the term *charisma* is employed in this study, and not in the more dilute sense in which some contemporary writers deploy it.

Weber gave first place to the supernatural in his characterization of the concept, and the term itself stands in direct continuity with its Christian theological sense of a gift of divine grace.

Primitive societies provided congenial milieux for charismatic leadership, although they are not the contexts classically cited in this connection. In this study, the classical locations of charisma are not discussed; instead modern social contexts are contrasted with primitive societies, in an attempt to open debate on the social milieux in which charisma might flourish or decline. Modern claims to supernatural power have a very different role and different implications, of course, but the contrast with the primitive world provides the opportunity, through the prism of charisma, to examine some of the characteristics of modern society. But these differences can be appreciated only if we hold the concept of charisma constant. Thus, part of the preliminary discussion in this essay seeks to show that some contemporary usage of the term is in fact misusage. My suggestions, therefore, are that it is useful to retain the term in the strong sense in which I use it, and desirable to reject the loose, popular, and perhaps even ideological attribution of "charisma" to leaders of any and all sorts, and to those who are no more than colourful or exuberant personalities.

The utility of the concept implies the reality of the phenomenon—not the phenomenon of divinely inspired men, but of the historical reality of widespread belief in such men and in the transcendent nature of their endowment with power. That belief is an important social fact, and a force in social development. That few of us today believe that individuals ever received divine power, or that there are radical, supernaturally determined unequal distributions of competence among men, reveals an irony. Many men in the past have believed in superhuman nobility. It was always an illusion: yet men needed to believe. Of course, they believed it to be rare—this combination of exceptional qualities, such as bigness of spirit, generosity, daring, courage, dignity, self-esteem, self-possession, openness, honesty, consideration of others, and, in the best unsqueamish sense, sensitivity. In some measure, many men possess some of these virtues, but the recognition of them as a *Gestalt* has perhaps occurred only where a supernatural source has been imputed.

My analysis suggests that such a belief is fully and widely credible only in pre-modern societies, in which the workings of the physical universe, and the structure of social organization itself are understood only in mythical terms. Charisma is ancient myth, and the reflection of man's primitive, in the sense also of primary, yearnings. Part of the paradox is that in simple societies, not only was there no alternative to reposing trust in a man as the agent of social transformation or as the saviour from prevailing miseries, but, in those conditions, such a man, in a way no longer true in the modern world, had some chance, however slight, of actually achieving something. Of course, *we* know that it was not so much the man as the faith of his followers that made them whole. But in the modern world, with its cumulative rationality and machine technology, a man is a much less plausible instrument. Then, a man could make the difference because moral solutions,

solutions in terms of appropriate attitudes and behaviour, might still work. We live in a post-moral age, in which the rights and wrongs of behaviour are increasingly determined by purely technical considerations. In this sense, too, then, the appeal of charisma, of the man whose supernatural nobility and power would save us, is primitive.

Yet charisma is part of our tradition, a romantic idea from the remote past that is always available for reactivation, even if, today, that occurs in only limited and peripheral areas of social activity. It retains its emotional attraction, it is simple to understand, and it appeals to the sheer human-ness of man as an utterly radical alternative to the oppressiveness of advanced technological society, whether capitalist or socialist.

The paradox of charisma is precisely the attraction of faith in man, the element of personal trust that has, in so many respects become either redundant or increasingly difficult in the modern world. It is reassertion of faith in human virtues and dispositions that, if supernatural, yet are also apparently natural—natural, that is, because not technological. They appear as uncompromised, either by the arduous effort that has to be undertaken to acquire them in everyday life, or by the conditions in which they are exercised. Faith is easier than empirical analysis, innate nobility a more congenial idea than cultivated learning, particularly when learning has turned away from the old, nineteenth-century belief in the cultivation of inner resources to the modern demand for instrumental expertise and calculated skills for use in a rational system.

Always rare enough to provoke intimations of the

supernatural (or to be attributable because of independent claims tò divine inspiration), nobility becomes an anachronism in the modern world. It is not the product of our socialization procedures, educational systems, psychological theories, or techniques of social selection. It has ceased even to be regarded as a possible pinnacle of human endeavour. It persists only as a disposition of faith, for those, at the social margins, with the will to believe in something that is in origin primitive.

I should not have written this essay if I did not believe in the value of looking at the concept of charisma, and of allowing the thoughts which it stimulates to engage our attention both in the interpretation of the past and in our understanding of the present. As I see it, charisma is a concept with its own inbuilt ambivalences: in discussing it, I hope to have avoided additional ambiguities of my own making.

Acknowledgements

Not for the first time, I find myself indebted to my friend, Teddy Schuller, for helping me to bring an embryonic idea to more rapid maturation than would have occurred without his interest and encouragement. My readers have been spared some errors and many lapses of style by the care with which the typescript was read by my friend and colleague, Terence Bull, who also read the proofs. I thank Mrs. Rona Koretz, not only for typing the manuscript, but also for her unfailing patience when an author changed his mind.

I

Charismatic Leadership: The Rehabilitation of a Concept

Weber's three types of legitimation of authority are intended, as are all ideal-type constructs, to have a "timeless" quality. But they are also clearly of unequal incidence in different historical periods. All ideal-types are constructed only after some, usually very considerable, acquaintance with empirical material. The cases that inform the charismatic type of legitimation of authority are drawn mainly from pre-modern society—the ancient Near East and the pre-feudal and feudal periods of European history. In our own times, charisma is a quality imputed to few political leaders. In popular use, the terms *charisma* and *leadership* have generally become disjoined: *charisma,* as the word has come to be used, connotes appeal more than it connotes authority. Even in the religious field, where there is most direct continuity with Israelitish prophetism, on which the concept draws so heavily, new styles of leadership emerge: the modern *guru* makes charismatic claims, but his charisma is not of the strong type attributed of old to prophets.[1]

1. Weber recognized different types of charisma. That of the guru is clearly charisma that "may be produced artificially by

In modern times, charismatic leadership persists only in the interstices between institutional orders, in the narrow social space that remains for collective behaviour, spontaneous faith, and unconstrained obedience and adulation. *Within* the institutional arrangements of society—and politics and religion are traditionally the areas most receptive—charisma persists only as a shadowy item. In politics, it sits uneasily in a system of procedures in which rationality is increasingly emphasized. Democratic representation; the assumption that men know their interests; the (at least apparent) fairness of electoral arrangements; the growing dominance of bureaucratic procedures within political parties, as well as within states, for the direction of which the parties compete—all leave a diminished place for the charismatic claimant. The political scientists maintain a hidden campaign (at times but thinly veiled) against what they see as irrational elements in the political system, emphasizing the possibility of "rational" choices, and excoriating "deference"; "ethnic prejudice"; "backlash"; and, by implication, "charisma." There is a residual acknowledgement of the marginal importance of the personal qualities of political candidates, and more particularly of those who contend for leadership positions—perhaps because

---

some extraordinary means. Even then it is assumed that charismatic powers can be developed only in people and objects in which the germ already existed but would have remained dormant unless evoked by some ascetic or other regimen." Max Weber, *The Sociology of Religion,* trans. Ephraim Fischer (London: Methuen, 1964), p. 2.

there are no other, more objective, criteria on which to make choices. But even here, it is assumed that charisma is something that the "image-makers," publicists, journalists, and backroom party hacks can manufacture. The term *charisma* is, of course, often used, especially by the journalists, but it is none the less widely conceded that contemporary politicians are lack-lustre, often mediocre men compared to those of former times (whom history books have made into giants). The basic trend is clear. As modern parties are bureaucratized; as political decisions are subject to more explicitly technical considerations; and as, in consequence, party political differences diminish, only the projected images of leadership and a few, often empty, shibboleths serve to distinguish one party from another.

The contemporary residual charismatic claims, manufactured as they often are, are then but a pale memory of the claims of those of the prophet or the heroic warrior. If there is a charismatic element in contemporary political systems, it is there only because of the impossibility of using strictly technical, economic, or scientific standards in determining ultimate preferences, or in deciding between personality types, the affective qualities of men, and the images that they project (or have projected for them). The relation of this to the acceptance by faith of claims to superiority of a supernatural kind is that of an attenuated residue. That ancient claim is possible only in a social context that sustains the credibility of supernatural power, a context in which the "solutions" to social problems, and salvation from destruction, are envisaged as necessarily the result of the intervention of the spirit, the god, or the man acting with god-endowed power.

A Concept and Its Corruption

Weber employed the term *charisma* in direct derivation of the idea of a gift of grace, extending the term to the endowment of an individual with supernatural power in any religious tradition, context, or culture.

> The term "charisma" will be applied to a certain quality of an individual personality by virtue of which he is set apart from ordinary men and treated as endowed with supernatural, superhuman, or at least specifically exceptional powers or qualities. These are such as are not accessible to the ordinary person, but are regarded as of divine origin or as exemplary, and on the basis of them the individual concerned is treated as a leader. . . . It is often thought of as resting on magical powers. How the quality in question would be ultimately judged from any ethical, aesthetic, or other such point of view is naturally entirely indifferent for purposes of definition. What is alone important is how the individual is actually regarded by those subject to charismatic authority, by his "followers" or "disciples".[2]

He repeats this final point, in saying, "It is recognition on the part of those subject to authority which is decisive for the validity of charisma." [3] Thus only those whose claim to supernatural power is recognized are

2. Max Weber, *Theory of Social and Economic Organization,* trans. A. R. Henderson and Talcott Parsons (Edinburgh: Hodge, 1947), p. 329.
   3. *Ibid.,* p. 330.

charismatic. Recognition, belief in the claims to supernatural power, is an integral element of charisma. Although charismatic leaders may need to manifest particular qualities—to perform miracles, or to demonstrate ecstasy—charisma is not a personality attribute, it is the social recognition of a claim. Charisma is a social phenomenon, not a psychological personality type.[4]

Claims to supernatural power may be of many types, and Weber distinguished several. He made it clear that charisma in what we shall term the strong sense, the charisma of the prophet, differed from the "charisma held by technicians of routine cults."[5] In primitive societies in particular, charismatic claims might be divided among chiefs, warriors, and magicians. But these were all different types of charisma from the charisma of the prophet, who, though he might use magic to validate his charismatic claims, was unlike the magician in claiming definite revelations, and in making doctrine and commandments the core of his concern, not merely the performance of

4. In making one distinction between two types of charisma, Weber wrote, "Charisma may be either of two types. Where the appellation is fully merited charisma is a gift that inheres in an object or person simply by virtue of natural endowment. Such primary charisma cannot be acquired by any means." *The Sociology of Religion,* p. 2. It might appear that Weber here refers to charisma as a personality attribute. But this could only be so if one supposed that Weber himself believed in the innate charisma of all the individuals (and objects) in the many and various societies for whom it has been successfully claimed.

5. *Ibid.,* p. 66. The process of routinization of charisma, and the phenomenon of charisma of office, fall outside the concerns of this book.

magical acts.[6] Prophets were the enunciators of new
prescripts for their societies. It is prophets, not magicians, who demand obedience, and it is of them that
terms such as *heroism* and *exemplary qualities* are employed. It is in them that *personal trust* is reposed.
When Weber discusses charisma without specific applications it appears to be prophets and perhaps heroic
warriors whom he has principally in mind.[7]

That the relationship between prophet and followers is problematic has been made clear by Bendix:
followers expect signs of power, but the demand for
absolute faith and obedience precludes their asking for
such. He writes, ". . . genuine charisma is a rare
event, born . . . of a belief in the mysterious gift of
one man which that man shares with those who follow
him." [8] The rarity is attributable to the delicacy of the
balance between leader and led in their demands for
signs from the one and faith from the other. The relation is one of supreme personal trust.

The rarity of the phenomenon must be contrasted
with the popularity of the term. Even sociologists have
come to use the word *charisma* in a very weak sense.
Almost as if taking their cues from the mass media,
they employ the term as if it referred simply to some
extraordinary, above-average, personal competence.
This is a long way from Weber's usage, and a curious
secularization of a term the origin of which is in the

6. *Ibid.*, pp. 47–48.

7. E.g., *Social and Economic Organization,* p. 301.

8. Reinhard Bendix, "Charismatic Leadership," in R. Bendix
and Gunther Roth, *Scholarship and Partisanship: Essays on Max
Weber* (Berkeley and Los Angeles: University of California Press,
1971), p. 187.

idea of supernatural endowment. The "charismatic personality" is, from a Weberian point of view, almost a contradiction in terms, and is certainly a debasement of the linguistic coinage. It represents an insensitivity to the very subtleties to which Weber was seeking to make us alert. Weber's concept, *charisma,* denotes a quality not of the individual, but of a relationship between believers (or followers) and the man in whom they believed. His claim, or theirs on his behalf, was that he had authority because of his supernatural competences. Charisma is not a personality attribute, but a successful claim to power by virtue of supernatural ordination. If a man runs naked down the street proclaiming that he alone can save others from impending doom, and if he immediately wins a following, then he is a charismatic leader: a social relationship has come into being. If he does not win a following, he is simply a lunatic.

Failure to distinguish the sociological concept from personality attributes is at the core of a number of corrupt or dilute applications of the term. It is arbitrary and potentially misleading to argue that charisma—once a scarce and special and very occasional phenomenon in society—has now been incorporated into many normal, routine functionings of the social system. To refer to individuals who enjoy some measure of marginal prestige in the eyes of their fellows and who have a reputation for reliability and competence as "charismatic" is an instance of this dilution. Foremen, supervisors, managers, may all require something above average in drive, *esprit,* personality, or—to put it closer to the charismatic—a capacity to stimulate

others and to summon their responses.[9] But these attributes are personal qualities, on the basis of which
good social relationships may rest. They may be indispensable to some courses of human action, and even to
some complex technical operations: but no element of
the supernatural is involved. This capacity is merely a
personality trait that is recognized in the respect and
standing that are accorded. Such a quality may be an
important social "lubricant." The goodwill of such
men, although not contracted for by employers, may
indeed be indispensable for many technical and com-
mercial activities. And it may be that we lack an adequate concept for the difference between "bigness of
spirit" which inspires confidence in one man, and that
poorness of spirit which makes us think very little of
another. The smooth running of affairs in technical or
bureaucratic systems may depend on more than technical, bureaucratic, and rational procedures. But it is a
long step from saying this to suggesting that they rely
on the diffusion of a supernatural capacity of which
many agents are possessed.[10] The persistence of the

9. In making this point, I differ completely from the usage
followed by Amitai Etzioni, *A Comparative Analysis of Complex Organizations* (New York: Free Press, 1961). See his discussion of
charisma in organizational positions, pp. 203–262.

10. The contrast of attributing charisma to foremen and managers and Weber's usage is clear from the following quotations:
"Charismatic authority is . . . specifically outside the realm of
every-day routine and the profane sphere. In this respect, it is
sharpy opposed both to rational, and particularly bureaucratic,
authority. . . . Both rational and traditional authority are specifically forms of every-day routine control of action; while the
charismatic type is the direct antithesis of this." ". . . charismatic authority is specifically irrational in the sense of being foreign

extra-rational may be vital to the maintenance of rational systems, and, if this is so, it is well to recognize the fact. Analysis is not facilitated, however, by assimilating this phenomenon to that of charisma. Nor are the qualities at issue confined to managerial classes: they may be no less important for social relationships at all levels.

Nor is charisma to be seen as merely a capacity for innovation even though innovation may always be part of the charismatic claim. More is involved in the concept than the recognition that whereas most men are conservators of their social roles, a few initiate and innovate. The charismatic figure certainly claims to possess qualities prized by at least some sections of society, and offers attractive prospects of renewal. But he is more than a mere innovator. He is necessarily also a romantic, a disruptor of the prevailing order, a man who abrogates and transcends convention, who creates discord, coming, as it were, to put the world to the sword.

The result of his activity is never immediately a contribution to social order: nor is it merely the begetter of order who is admired in society. Those admired to

to all rules. . . . It recognizes no appropriation of positions of power by virtue of the possession of property. . . . The only basis of legitimacy for it is personal charisma, so long as it is proved; that is, as long as it receives recognition and is able to satisfy the followers or disciples. But this lasts only so long as the belief in its charismatic inspiration remains." "Pure charisma is specifically foreign to economic considerations." "From the point of view of rational economic activity, charisma is a typical antieconomic force. It repudiates any sort of involvement in the every-day routine world." Max Weber, *Social and Economic Organization,* pp. 332–333.

the point of seeming godlike, or who claim to speak in the name of the supernatural, must be greater than their context, offering new possibilities, stimulating new visions of a social order very different from the present. Charisma, as Weber conceived it, implied a definite break in the previously existing structure of social and power relationships.[11] Such breaks demand divisions and rivalries; they entail a breach of existing moral imperatives.

Shils writes, "The charismatic propensity is a function of the need for order. The generator or author of order arouses charismatic responsiveness."[12] Certainly, prophets may see their task as being to "rearrange the world," and often they promise a new pattern of perhaps faultless order, but one cannot ignore the powerful thrust for change and transformation which prophecy also implies, and change, at least in the short run, must mean disorder. There is no *prime facie* reason to suppose that all innovative power must contribute to the smooth working of systems. Nor is it apparent why only expansive, impressive personalities should be labelled charismatic. Certainly, if the claimant to charismatic leadership is a man possessed of distinctive social virtues, this may help the relationship of faith which charismatic leadership entails: none the less, if men can believe that an individual possesses God's gift of grace, they can also believe that medioc-

11. In *Economy and Society* (New York: Bedminster Press, 1968), p. 241, Weber refers to charisma as the greatest revolutionary power in periods of established tradition.

12. Edward Shils, "Charisma, Order, and Status," *American Sociological Review,* 30 (April, 1965): 199–213.

rity is excellence. For each Adonis-like James Nayler, there has probably also been a wizened, lack-lustre Smyth-Piggott: but each was accepted as a messiah.[13] Successful charismatic leaders are often believed to be possessors of exceptional virtues (of which expansiveness may be one) but often, such virtues are themselves only part of the myth of charisma. Nobility *may* be inherent in the charismatic claimant, but often it is only a pale reflection of the nobility that is claimed.

Quite apart from the inconvenience of the debasement of the sociological coinage which contemporary applications of the concept of charisma entail, there appears to me to be another objection to current usage. To suggest that charisma is involved in the maintenance of order, promotes regulated innovation, and sustains a pliant and readily accommodated spirit of innovation in the prevailing social order, appears to fall not far short of using the concept as an ideological defence. It is to argue that, despite all appearances to the contrary, the attractive aspects of the nonrational, personal, individual, and spontaneous persist in contemporary society. Despite the rigour of modern technology and bureaucracy, the inhumanity, facelessness, and relentlessness of the system—so much the focus of the criticism of the young—"charisma," itself a charm word, is said to be deeply involved in it all. The prison-house of bureaucratic society, that Weber foresaw as the destiny of twentieth-century man, is not a

13. Nayler was the Bristol leader of the Quakers, who entered the city riding on a donkey, and was regarded by his followers as the messiah. Smyth-Piggott was a latter-day self-styled messiah who presided over a small commune in Somerset, England.

prison-house after all, but is itself the arena for the more extended exercise of distinctively human attributes.

The new application of the concept appears, then, to be an attempt to reassert faith in the individual, implying an area of operation for human free will, which mitigates the inexorability of the system by the deployability of unconstrained and uncontracted personality attributes. To suggest that it is charisma—not science or rational procedures—which really makes the wheels go round, is to resuscitate an emphasis on the individual for which Weber's critics took him rather too severely to task. Using an unduly strong term to describe what is a marginal, peripheral, and intersticial phenomenon, is one way of overstating a case. Neither of the two principal exponents of the thesis that charisma persists as an important element in modern life uses the concept to suggest that the idea of the specifically supernatural is retained in modern life. Nor is it used by them as a way of contending particularly against the secularization thesis.[14] They do, however, appear to use it as a type of defence of the capitalist, liberal, democratic social system. That system depends on effective bureaucratic control, but bureaucracy is its least enchanting facet, and as the depen-

14. Sociologists who reject the secularization thesis might easily have used arguments about the persistence of charisma, given the lead of Shils and Etzioni. But while these last-named do not appear to wish to harness their argument about the persistence of charisma to the persistence of religion, opponents of the secularization thesis (Robert Bellah, Thomas Luckmann, and David Martin, for example) do not seem to be impressed by the evidence for the persistence of charisma in the religious sphere.

dence grows so opposition to the system itself in-
creases. If only the importance of personal virtues can
be reasserted (and I do not dispute their importance or
their desirability) then the impersonality of routine
procedures may, at least in theory, be mitigated. The
bureaucratic world is to be re-enchanted—by emphasizing the diffusion of charisma throughout the system. Charisma is at once more attractive than legal-ra-
tional authority: the democratization of the concept is
itself an interesting phenomenon in the sociology of
(sociological) knowledge. I am unconvinced that its
use assists us in the analysis of contemporary society.

A Concept to be Abandoned?

Despite these strictures on the extension of the use
of the concept of charisma, and its application to qualities that seem to me to bear but the faintest resem-
blance to those that are attributed to divine inspiration, I am far from persuaded that the concept of
charisma ought to be abandoned. It is the fate of sociological concepts to suffer debasement. Sociology itself
is an attempt not merely to express important aspects
of social reality at a particular time; it is also an in-
terpretative exercise. As such, sociology is always
engaged in reinterpreting society in every age—and
since there are many interpreters there is no consensus.
Sociology has a much less cumulative character than
the natural sciences; much less than they, can it be expected to arrive at anything approaching definitive
positions. It must experience, through the wide acceptance within society of particular sociological interpre-

tations at a particular time, the loss of rigour and precision in the use of concepts that are picked up and vulgarized. Charisma, of all sociological concepts, has experienced such popularization.

This development should be distinguished from the one already discussed, in which the concept has been used in a much diluted sense. Popularization is the process by which the concept has passed into general currency as a designation of the personality attributes of well-regarded public figures. Charisma is not the power possessed by a young, vigorous, and idealistic political leader. The journalists who use the term, are a little removed in their use of it from the adulators of ancient worthies, warriors, or prophets, who saw the divine spark in the eyes of their leaders and who claimed charisma for them by virtue of it. The difference is that the journalists *use* the term charisma, even though they entirely misunderstand the social relationship that it expresses, and misapply it in describing the mysterious quality of leadership, attributing it *to the man* rather than to the public's belief in him. (That in so doing they may create such a relationship—may indeed hope to do so—is not at issue.)

Commenting on this development, Peter Worsley has declared that charisma is too "spongy" a concept to be of further use in sociology. Sensitive to the fact that charisma is a function of recognition, he is also aware that the process by which approval or consent is elicited and conferred is necessarily a complex one. Writing from a Marxist perspective, Worsley is suspicious of the idea of charisma. While he perceives the essentially social quality of charisma too well to charge

Weber with using the concept in order to facilitate a reassertion of the great man theory of history, none the less it is not to the effect of (misplaced) belief in the power of leaders that Worsley is disposed to look for explanations of historical processes. He regards the loyalty of followers and the qualities of leaders as marginal items in the explanation of social movements and their consequences. He is more impressed by the quality of the message and its appropriateness to the dawning conception of the rights and interests of particular exploited classes.[15]

The particular social movements dealt with in his book—to the second edition of which he added a preface on charismatic leadership—were movements among peoples at very simple levels of social development. In Melanesia, although a type of achieved status was well known and hereditary chieftainship was not the normal pattern, the status of the "self-made" man was intimately connected with the individual's abilities as a producer of foodstuffs and trade goods, as an economic organizer at the level of domestic economy, rather than as a military, political, or spiritual genius.[16] Thus there was, even traditionally, little room for a conception of the charismatic: the "big man" of Melanesian society was too easily explained in common-sense terms to require ideas of divine afflatus. It is as well to note that Worsley is not concerned with

15. Peter Worsley, *The Trumpet Shall Sound,* 2nd ed. (New York: Schocken, 1968), introduction.

16. For a discussion of the role of the "big man," see Glynn Cochrane, *Big Men and Cargo Cults* (Oxford: Clarendon Press, 1970).

the typical contexts that interested Max Weber: his rejection of the concept of charisma stems from a study in societies to which Weber made no reference.

In Melanesian cultural conditions, social movements and upsurges might be explained without the use of the concept of charisma. Worsley maintained that in those cultures local exemplifications of an act of faith in some man of superordinate power was a rarity or was absent (although certainly there was often dependence on local "big men"). Extraordinary social power was not claimed by reference to the divine, perhaps because power differentials between individuals were not sufficiently great to warrant appeal to exceptional sources (other than those of conventional sorcery ideas). But whatever the Melanesian evidence might be, it does not in itself establish a case against the utility of the concept of charisma in other cultural times and places. To show that in these very simple societies men—though misapprehending causes, and though still being in the thrall of magical patterns of thinking—none the less act in some sense in ways suggested by their "real" interests, is not to show that men may not, in other epochs or locales, act for different ends and on very different assumptions about the ultimate source of their satisfactions.

The Melanesians were, and remain, preoccupied with trade goods: their cultural style is dominated by the accumulation of foodstuffs and the acquisition of possessions, many of which are wanted for purposes of very specific activities of exchange, and in the maintenance of very specific relationships, but all of which are wanted for their value in the enhancement of status.

These cultural preoccupations come close—despite the absence of systematic social stratification or class relationships, and with only rudimentary application of the concept of changing techniques of production—to economic determinist expectations about social organization. Local preoccupation with economic pursuits, and the dependence of personal status on economic competence, give at least an appearance of plausibility to the idea that cargo cults among Melanesians represent a paradigm case of prepolitical class consciousness.

Yet the cases are also very different in several crucial dimensions, and not only because of the absence in Melanesia of any well-articulated political self-consciousness. Local wealth is of very discrete types, accumulated in particular specie with restricted exchange purposes. The achieved status of "big men" in Melanesian societies lacks connotations for social stratification: it is a personal accomplishment without even that hereditary dimension that adds some measure of permanence in diversity of life-styles, life-opportunities, and primary advantages that characterize particular social classes in Western society, and chieftainship and aristocracy in some traditional African societies. By straining the analogy somewhat, one might see traders, planters, and colonial administrators as one class and natives as another, but differences among and within local "tribal" groups must lead to serious emendation of this analogy. Again, there are many examples of outbursts of cargo cult enthusiasm that affect one village and not another, which, within a Marxist framework of reasoning, would be difficult to explain except by making implausible assumptions of differential class consciousness and divergent perceptions of "real" interests. Outside this framework they are easily explained—as arising from the local prestige of prominent individuals who persuade, or dissuade, their neighbours in respect of particular cult activities. Again, there are instances of cargo cults breaking out, with attendant hysteria in societies not previously in touch with Europeans—which is to say in societies in which no exploitation has occurred and in which all that has happened is the antecedent rumour of the coming of the white man.[17] In such an instance a theory of the disruptive effects of even anticipatory cultural contact and apprehension of the consequences of being brought into close proximity with extraordinary, apparently superordinate power, suggests a more cogent line of argument than explanations based on economic determinism.[18]

It must be conceded, that explanation of cargo cults in terms of the emotional disorder created by cultural contact does not in itself imply a theory of charismatic leadership: but it does not conflict with it, and it does require that we acknowledge the importance of *local* apprehension of supernatural power.[19] That apprehen-

17. Ronald Berndt, "Reaction to Conquest in the Eastern Highlands of New Guinea," *Oceania* 24 (March and June, 1954): 190–228, 255–274.

18. For a discussion of the limitations of economic determinist analysis in this respect, see Lucy Mair, "The Pursuit of the Millennium in Melanesia," *British Journal of Sociology* IX, 2 (June, 1958): 175–182.

19. This type of theory, without much reference to the role of charisma, is expounded in Bryan R. Wilson, *Magic and the Millennium* (London: Heinemann, and New York: Harper and Row, 1973).

their loyalty. Quite often, the initiators of such rumours are adolescents or feeble-minded individuals—both categories of people who are only partially socialized, and who would not normally command a hearing. They are often no more than the momentary recipients of a divine apprehension and they are thereafter relatively little regarded. The message appears to be of more importance than the medium in these cases.

Yet what must not be lost sight of, is that in such societies, and also in societies at much higher levels of development, and in particular sections even of state societies, there is a persistent tendency to interpret social relationships and social organization in essentially personal terms. It is not only that the gods (or God) are seen as individual beings—like men in all essential respects, in their mental functioning and in their motivations—but that to these agents is ascribed a wide range of power over the natural and social orders. Even where completely impersonal agencies exist, such as the bureaucratic structures of more advanced societies, there is a tendency to anthropomorphize them. This is not the sophisticated point of the methodological individualist, of the Max Weber who recognizes that every complex social system—church, state, bureaucracy, army—is ultimately no more than an arrangement of human actions, albeit a complex, sustained, and immensely elaborated structure of action. What is involved is a more simplistic apprehension of how things work—the idea that if things are happening, then there must be identifiable persons who are causing them to happen. A simple model of interpersonal relations, with which men are acquainted in their everyday affairs, is projected on to all social events, processes, and structures, and often also on to all natural phenomena too. If all sections and events proceed from volitions, then nature, demographic facts, social organization, custom, economic procedures all appear to be subject to the effective control of particular superordinate beings. Although men seek to constrain nature, and to impose their own wills, much that happens in society, economy, and polity is beyond their control. For those whose horizons are narrowly circumscribed, there is a tendency to suppose that particular agents organize society and can control its affairs as they choose. The child in our own society may refuse to believe that its father cannot repair a defective television set, and may see his failure to do so as a willful, spiteful act. The individual living unreflectively in a society in which the powers of generalization and abstraction are low—and such might still be the case in some of the less-developed subcultures of our own society—may naively believe in the near omnipotence of politicians and potentates, believe that they are above the law, do as they like, wield far more extensive power than is in fact the case. ("Why do they allow . . ."; "they ought to make a law . . ."; "what is the government thinking about . . ." are the recurrent everyday terms in which this attitude finds some expression.)

In simple societies this personification of power is much more common. In societies in which men have a limited range of often rather similar experiences, abstract categories of thought are unnecessary for everyday explanations, and are in any case unattainable. The powerful man is known as such, and the explanation of his power needs no analysis of social circumstances: the facts of consent in, and acceptance of, power are not intellectually visible. Power is itself a force and is manifested in particular personages. Furthermore, it is a force that is experienced: the powerful man is the man whose power one feels; one trembles, feels abashed, and one believes that these emotional responses *prove* that his power is an objective fact. This circular hypothetical process of emotional reasoning is self-sustaining. No other hypotheses are necessary to explain power apart from this attribution of its source and nature. In such simple societies the explanatory process is of course not of this kind. Nature is understood, we are told, "in the personal idiom," and there is reason to suppose that society and its processes are understood in the same way. Thinking "in the personal idiom" has been represented as the principal difference between Western scientific thinking and African "religious" thinking.[21] It is, however, a very big difference, and it rules out immediately the possibility of objective detachment, the separation of the cognitive operation of the mind from the emotional and evaluative functions, on which Western natural sciences and, in considerable measure, the social sciences, depend.

As a mode of thought, "the personal idiom" implies the sustained social involvement of known individuals. It is also of the essence of magical and religious thinking, and it might even be seen as characterizing artistic

21. Robin Horton, "African Traditional Thought and Western Science," *Africa* 37, 1 and 2 (January and April, 1967): 50–71, 155–187.

endeavour, in contrast with the cold, detached, impersonal style of Western science. The artist's view must always be "a personal view"; the scientist's must never be. "The personal idiom" has an implication which is not without its immediate appeal: it suggests that social relationships in societies in which thought is of this kind, are relationships of personal trust. Relations are between total individuals, not between segmentary role performers as is the case in advanced societies, in which the total individual is almost an abstraction—a reconstruction of the numerous and diverse role performances in which he is involved. In advanced societies, the individual's affective sentiments are little if at all engaged in his many segmentary involvements. He is an agent, most of whose relations are confined to specific contractual activities. The element of trust in these relations is in specific skills, qualifications, competences, and performances. Man as man is involved only in the most remote and generalized sense in most of these roles, insofar as they depend on his underlying goodwill to perform at a given time and place—and this willingness is itself underwritten as part of the pecuniary contract for role performances.

Societies where experience, knowledge, and received wisdom can be expressed in the personal idiom are societies in which it is impossible, or possible in very limited degree, to distinguish a man from his particular role performances. There is as yet no social need for such a distinction. Nor is there a necessity to separate knowledge of the man from judgments and evaluations about him. There is an inextricable involvement of a man's factual attributes with the evaluation of them, and with the emotional responses that they arouse. The individual is in effect looked upon as a total indivisible being. The condition for seeing all of one's fellow men as total beings is to live in a society with a low degree of role differentiation, a circumstance which precludes all the enrichments that we regard as the fruit of civilization.

A broad distinction may be drawn between hypothetical polar types of society: that organized through a high degree of specificity of role performances; and that composed of total persons. The distinction has many analogues in sociological theory, but this particular focus makes apparent the conduciveness to charismatic phenomena of particular social contexts. Charisma is a relation of supreme trust in the total competence of an individual, whose qualities are "supernatural, superhuman, or at least specifically exceptional." Charisma is the extreme exemplification of thinking in a personal idiom. But there must be certain other social preconditions before charisma, in a socially significant sense—in the Weberian sense—is manifested. In very simple societies, comprising small, relatively isolated units of nomadic hunters, there have sometimes been charismatic claims, but the scale of social intercourse is here too limited, the room for charismatic manoeuvre too confined, for prophecy to obtain much purchase on the social situation (even though it may thoroughly grip the minds and hearts of men). Socially significant charisma appears to require a particular scale of relationships, an incipient prospect at least for a radical division of functions between men, as commander and commanded, and a prospect of reordering these relationships by some new principles.

The Occasions for Charisma

Weber saw charisma as providing a break in existing social relationships. Although ephemeral in its incidence, and lacking a stable basis for a persisting form of authority, charisma challenges the existing order. It operates to break the existing authority structure, to lift sanctions on previously proscribed behaviour, and to promise men new freedoms—but it is also the occasion on which new men make new claims to obedience. Whether there were any charismatic movements in nonliterate societies before such societies were known to outside (usually Western) observers, is clearly difficult to establish. Natural catastrophes, famine, plague, or drought may have provided such occasions, but the most frequently observed circumstances of charismatic phenomena appear to be the conditions promoted by wars or the clash of cultures. Invasions or migrations may have caused disruption of norms and values from time to time, creating occasions on which men might have accepted the offer of extraordinary supernatural intervention had it been available.

Western incursions into the territory of such societies probably persisted longer and manifested greater disparity of power between indigenes and invaders than those occurring in earlier epochs, but the incidence of prophetism among the Jews in the Egyptian or Babylonian captivities, or under the Greek and

Roman conquerors, suggests that the mere scale of the divergences in technical competence, then so much less, is not the primary source of that failure within a culture that stimulates charismatic phenomena or receptiveness to them. Charisma is undoubtedly a cause of social change: but it also appears to be a response to it, a response to social disruption.

It is perhaps misleading to suppose that the hypothetical state that we call "normal times" (and it is a concept that for ordinary purposes we can scarcely do without) were ever of long duration in any historical period. It is easier for us to suppose that relatively small scale preliterate societies may for long periods have survived in relatively unchanging conditions. In such circumstances it is perhaps warranted to suppose that the charismatic phenomenon would be uncommon, unless—and the condition is important—the charismatic impulse is already part of the cultural tradition. Once charismatic leadership has occurred among a people, it is capable of periodic recrudescence, and may, apparently, be reactivated without the experience of new processes of social change, which appear to be the first stimulant of charismatic claims. Once the myth of the charismatic leader exists within a social tradition, then the myth itself becomes an element of social reality, capable of influencing subsequent developments.

Thus it could well be that the shamans who have been active for some centuries among the bands of Tupi-Guaraní Amerindian peoples of Brazil, may have reasserted a claim to divine power from time to time more on the impulse of tradition than in response to specific social conditions. The Tupi-Guaraní have become celebrated for the long migrations that bands of varying size undertook, and which, in modern times at least, appear to have been prompted essentially by religious motives, to march to the "land without evil" at the behest of a particular local visionary. The myth of such a place suggests the experience of conditions of social distress, but we do not know whether the distress was of recent and recurrent experience, or was long past, the recollection of which was powerful enough to give the shamans credibility when, from time to time, they reactivated the old response.[22]

Similarly, although the extent and even the existence of prophetism among simpler peoples before Western cultural contact is open to dispute, we do know of cases in which local prophets have arisen among small, relatively unacculturated, bands of savages when they have been faced with endemic warfare and continuing uncertainty about their life chances in relation to a superior enemy. But in the cases about which we know, prophetism of a superior sort has already been experienced. If the claims of a past prophet galvanized indigenes to action that seemed to be almost successful, then that memory might stimulate

22. On the Tupi-Guaraní, see Alfred Métraux, "The Tupinamba" and "The Guaraní" in *Handbook of South American Indians,* ed. Julian H. Steward, vol. III (Washington, D.C.: Smithsonian Institution, Bureau of American Ethnography Bulletin, 1948), pp. 69–94 and 95–133; Alfred Métraux, "Migrations historiques des Tupi-Guaraní," *Journal de la Société des Américanistes,* N.S. XIX (Paris, 1927): 1–45; W. H. Lindig, "Wanderungen der Tupi-Guaraní und Eschatologie der Apapocuva-Guaraní," in W. E. Mühlmann, *Chiliasmus und Nativismus* (Berlin: Reimer, 1961).

ideas of reinvoking supernatural aid. Great prophets are likely to have local imitators who prescribe specific courses of action and expression, violating old taboos and imposing new ones that are but little different from those enjoined by the great prophet. The difference between them is merely the scale of the group for whose "salvation" they profess to cater. Clearly, it is difficult to establish a firm distinction between great prophets and local prophets, and difficult to suggest that there ever is an original who truly initiates a tradition. But for present purposes we need do no more than point to differences in scale and effectiveness to substantiate the distinction, which is a distinction of importance for recognizing what I have termed "socially significant charisma," for distinguishing the occasions when charisma is a powerful element in social change and those when it is merely a derived recollection, an echo of greater possibilities on past occasions.

It is not implicit in the concept of charisma that we should suppose that great prophets are great men, or are indeed anything different as men from lesser prophets or even from other people. A charismatic leader must be a plausible vessel for divine grace: but the very content of "plausibility" is itself culturally determined. It may be more than average endowment of energy, determination, fanaticism, and perhaps intelligence. Or it may be an altogether different set of attributes—epilepsy, strangeness, what we should regard as a mental disorder, or, particularly where children are regarded as prophets, even sheer innocence. Often, in these last-mentioned instances, it is others who take up, magnify, and give social significance to the prophecy. Most of all, a prophet whose leadership is to last for very long, requires success—the fulfilment of the prophecies that he utters. (Which is not to deny that some "once only" prophecies that have failed have radically changed the course of a people's history.)

An instance of the feeble-minded prophet is found in Te Ua Haumene, who acquired plausibility by successfully prophesying the wreck of a ship, the *Lord Worsley,* off the coast of New Zealand.[23] On the basis of this reputation, the Hau Hau movement among the Maoris arose in opposition to the British in 1862. Te Ua's prophecy was the occasion for others to stimulate a religiously inspired rising, to follow the intermittent warfare that had already developed between the government and the tribes. Te Ua's case is none the less instructive. His prophecy was used to weld into alliance hitherto mutually hostile tribes, and was a more successful vehicle for that purpose than the enthronment of a Maori king—a device to which some tribes had already had recourse. A king was altogether too constitutionally conceived an authority to become the focus for Maori unity, which was itself predicated on the need for rebellion. The prophet was the other available model of a superordinate agent. Whereas the idea of a king was drawn directly from what Maoris had

23. On the Hau-Hau movement, see S. Barton Babbage, *Hauhauism: An Episode in the Maori Wars* (Wellington, N.Z.: A. H. and A. W. Reed, 1937); William Greenwood, "The Upraised Hand, or the Spiritual Significance of the Ringatu Faith," *Journal of the Polynesian Society* 51, 1 (March 1942): i–vi and 1–81; Robin W. Winks, "The Doctrine of Hau-Hauism," *Journal of the Polynesian Society* 62, 3 (September, 1953) 199–236.

learned of the British monarchy, the idea of the prophet was learned directly from the Old Testament, with which, by the 1860s, Maoris were well acquainted. Transcendent power from God might weld together the fissiparous tribal groups. Yet prophets are not produced to order, and when the Maoris stumbled on the alternative principle of authority (alternative to traditional claims to authority that is), the man who fortuitously came forward with prophecy was scarcely equal to the role. To know of Old Testament prophets, and to perceive the similarity of their own circumstance with that of the Jews in Babylon was not tantamount to reproducing appropriate cultural conditions for the emergence of the fully fledged prophet.

The significance of Te Ua's prophecy is that it indicates the point in a situation at which charismatic claims may be effectively made; it indicates the unifying function of prophecy in circumstances in which no other agencies could forge unity, in which no other claim could supervene to induce men to set aside local differences and enmities. And it indicates this all the more forcibly precisely because Te Ua was not himself a worthy claimant to charismatic authority.

Charisma in Preliterate Societies

Although he did not explicitly exclude them, preliterate societies were not among those to which Weber made specific allusion in his discussion of charisma. Given the mode of men's thinking in such societies, and their archetypical *gemeinschaftlich* character, one might expect, when the overwhelming disruption of conquest or invasion is experienced, that charisma might be a potential cultural resource of preliterate peoples. But such societies are often small in scale and embrace a very limited degree of role differentiation: hence the traditional differences in power between individuals is also likely to be of small degree. In such societies—in North America, New Zealand, Melanesia—the new claims to power may surpass the possibilities of each separate tribal group. Traditional groupings may then be transcended, new levels of social organization may be half glimpsed, or even ephemerally realized, towards the attainment of new collective ends. Although the consequences may not be sustained, as, for instance, in Middle Eastern charisma, from Jesus (and his tradition) to Muhammed (and his), none the less, the determining significance of the act of faith in the superordinate efficacy of one man as an agency of social change is clear.

Of course, the long-term effect of charisma in simple societies, whether in the lives that are touched by it, or in the changes in social organization, is understandably, not to be compared with the effects of a Jesus, or even of a Mahdi, or a Hung Hsiu-ch'üan. When God, or his younger brother, walked the earth—or when millions believe that he did—the claim is explicitly intended to change the course of known human history. In contrast, what is seen in the case of simple societies, is a social "jacking-up" operation, in which, through charisma, new levels of integration are attained, new purchase is obtained in the minds of men for the conception of society that men entertain. For such moments of change, charisma performs a function analogous to that posited for the totem in the static conditions of society: it provides an objectification by reference to which society can take cognizance of itself. In this instance, not social cohesion, but possibilities of new levels of power and of social integration are the matters at issue. By this act of faith in divine power, men unwittingly create a device by which new power relations may be forged. The paradox is implicit in all social relations, best expressed in the conundrum which asserts that while society is independent of its individual components, at the same time it exists only in the minds of men. So, by belief in the charismatic claim, the fact of charisma is brought into being. The latent functions of these collective social psychological processes are such, of course, that cannot be attained by rational and conscious planning: indeed, in the degree to which rationality and consciousness are present, so the latent functions of such collective representations appear to be precluded. (This paradox exercised the minds of the founders of sociology, of course: Weber, in the distinction between substantive and formal rationality; and Durkheim in search of rational substitutes for unconscious functions.)

It is precisely because the effects of charisma in preliterate societies are less readily institutionalized, are half grasped, and then let go, that the potential of this particular phenomenon can be most clearly recognized. In more advanced societies, the charismatic leader has interpreters who ensure the persistence of the new vision. They may, as in Christianity, spiritualize the charismatic vision, entirely transforming its pristine significance, and making from the highly disruptive messianic, chiliastic, and millennial prophecy the building-blocks for a new pattern of social order. In small preliterate societies such a process is precluded. The very dependence on personal trust, the absence of literate traditions, and the difficulty of sustaining long-run organization virtually destine charisma to failure. The expectation, among all simple-minded people, is that change should be "sudden and soon." In the nature of the case, all processes of social transformations are—relative to these expectations—gradual, entailing, as they do, the diffusion of new norms, processes of socialization, and the creation of supportative institutions. These phenomena, all of which are interrelated, provide effective resistance to those who would pull apart the web of custom: the problems are well enough known to those involved in development studies. The charismatic leader in the simple society is faced—unless completely deluded by his own visions and entirely expectant on supernatural intervention in man's affairs—with the basic problem of how to elicit sustained commitment for his immediately appealing message.

Thus, a further paradox presents itself in respect of charisma in simple societies: precisely because conditions appear to be in theory so good for the emergence of the charismatic—at least in respect of the basis of personal trust—so they are bad for the persistence of the achievement of the charismatic leader. And as Weber pointed out, the charismatic leader is always at the mercy of the demand that he produce the miracles that he has promised. To sustain commitment the charismatic must succeed, must at least produce the signs of wonders to come. In simple societies, even the extent of manipulation that is necessary to create the *appearance* of success, is limited, and, as we have seen, the possibilities of institutionalization are equally circumscribed.

Hence, it is altogether understandable that the existence of the charismatic in preliterate societies should be overlooked, since all those developments associated with the routinization of charisma are likely to be absent. What is more often referred to is merely the incidence of prophets, of deranged individuals, and this is so because the social consequences of the emergence of most of these figures is, at least in the long run, very slight. Furthermore, of course, the interpretation of the role of these figures has—thus far—always been made by administrators, settlers, or missionaries—or by historians who, on the basis of their evidence, have subsequently written the history of the figures and events at issue. Whilst they might accord charisma to the great figures in their own country's history, they may have been less perceptive of such social relationships in the case of newly emerging indigenous leaders, except perhaps where a latter-day element of romanticism has caught the imagination.

Thus, because the societies concerned were of small scale, without the social conditions for institutionalization, without the possibilities of local and internal reinterpretation of failure, or the manipulation of claims, and with written records available from the pens only of sceptics, the primitive hero is unlikely to establish himself as the fully fledged charismatic

leader. In small-scale preliterate societies, with their
low degree of differentiation, the persistence of the
belief in men of exceptional power, is unlikely to be
long sustained. The very conditions which allow a
leader to be isolated so that he may acquire legendary
stature are absent (just as, in very advanced societies,
communications are so good that isolation is difficult
for other reasons). Of course, in larger scale preliterate
societies, and particularly in the latter half of the twen-
tieth century, new possibilities for institutionalization
present themselves in societies but recently developed
from a preliterate past. Thus the charismatic claims
made on behalf of Simon Kimbangu in the Congo of
the 1920s are stabilized and institutionalized in the organization that has arisen to claim his prophetic inheritance—*Église de Jésus-Christ sur le Terre par le Prophète
Simon Kimbangu*. Slowly the relationships of personal
trust are themselves being transformed, and new sustaining mechanisms are evolved. Such movements,
too, acknowledge their institutionalization by the par-
tiality of their social constituency, as churches rather
than as nations, claiming the next world rather than
this one, and moderating the extent of their claims on
their follower's allegiance. Where such social conditions have not arisen, however, the likelihood, in preliterate societies faced with disruptive conditions, is
for charismatic claims to be ephemeral and, at best, recurrent.

2

Charismatic Leaders in Less-Developed Societies

The case studies that follow are intended to provide some indications of the conditions, occasions, and consequences of charisma in preliterate societies. Of necessity, all the cases arise in the context of extensive cultural contact between men from Western society and the men of preliterate societies, but at different stages during the course of that long-drawn-out process, the long-term consequence of which is the massive Westernization of the world. The object is not to discuss the direction in which such prophets and warrior heroes have sought to deploy the power they acquire. Thus the discussion is not concerned with nativism, revitalization, or acculturation, but with the devices by which commitment is summoned and allegiance commanded, and the effects on social organization of responses to such summonses. Nor is it the intention to provide brief vignettes of individual personalities—were such possible about the figures from remote cultures, and, often, from remote periods—but only to assess their social reputation, and their socially recognized or imputed qualities, which is the real measure of their "nobility."

Pontiac

The pattern of leadership among the Indians of the eastern part of North America was spasmodic, ephemeral, and uncertain. The hereditary principle did not govern chieftainship, and the wandering bands of tribesmen appear to have responded to the leadership of particular individuals, to younger men as war chiefs, and older ones as spokesmen and elders. No individual's leadership was for life, however, and rivalries, the relative smallness of living groups and their susceptibility to fission, all militated against the emergence of stable, persisting leaders. Assuredly, and most probably by dint of personality and perhaps family connections, certain individuals did acquire fearful reputations as the great chiefs of their particular tribes, to whom some sort of allegiance would be owed by a number of normally separate bands of hunters. The precise basis for such authority remains obscure, but throughout the accounts of the settlement of America, the names of certain commanding figures are known for a period of perhaps two decades, as the respected chiefs of whole tribal groups—Minavavana of the Chippewas, who was Pontiac's contemporary; Quanah Parker of the Comanches, about a century later; Sitting Bull, the great Hunkpapa Sioux, perhaps the best known of all.

But these leaders were not charismatic figures: their status did not depend on some claim to supernatural legitimation. They were rather the fathers of their particular people, and presumably earned that position at least in part by their particular personal qualities.

They were, despite the absence of a clear hereditary principle, the inheritors of a traditional type of authority. The charismatic leader was one who emerged, with supernatural justification, acquiring authority over a much less traditionally defined group, and usually to accomplish specific ends.

Although Indians were volatile, and—perhaps because hunting puts local and even individual skill and initiative at a premium—leadership as such was always tenuous, they were prepared in some measure and for some time to give heed to the leadership claims of extraordinary figures. Given the geographic dispersal of hunting people, it was not easy for one commanding individual to emerge as an effective leader: at the same time the same set of circumstances may have helped to magnify the attributes of a man as he became known to others at a distance. The terms in which a new leader might effectively claim allegiance must—if diverse groups were to be united in allegiance to him—necessarily invoke some superordinate reference point that placed him beyond the internal tribal divisiveness of the Indians. Mere "indian-ness" as such was perhaps not yet enough. Yet some appeal to the underlying cultural unity of red men was the only basis for such leadership.

Authority, then, had to be claimed in the archetypical charismatic style—from supernatural sources. Unfortunately, we do not know to what extent such a claim was by Pontiac's time already a possibility within the cultural tradition of North American Indians. Parkman comments, "the great susceptibilities of the Indian to superstitious impressions renders the

advent of a prophet among them no very rare occurrence." [1] That was certainly so in the mid-nineteenth
century when he was writing, and indeed long before
this. [2] By then the prophet was already a culturally
well-accepted possibility. We simply do not know,
and cannot know, whether the prophet was an indigenous phenomenon. What we do see, however, is that
there is a curious division of labour evident at this
time, and not only in the case of Pontiac's claim to authority, but also, four decades later, in that of the
Shawnee, Tecumseh. One man emerges as the
prophet, but it is another who uses prophecy to mobi-
lize a following. The faith in supernatural means is not
such, at least at this time, that the prophet himself
becomes the leader. The ends to which leadership is
directed are to be attained still by practical everyday
means, not by exclusive dependence on the supernatural. Hence the prophecy must be used by the warrior,
and it is the warrior who acquires the charismatic man-
tle provided by the prophet. Only at a later stage of
North American Indian history, when war is no longer
a realistic recourse in their relations with whites, even
in the Indian's own assessment of the circumstances,
does the prophet himself become the charismatic
leader. Such was the impressiveness of Pontiac as a

1. Francis Parkman, *The Conspiracy of Pontiac* (London: Mac-
millan 1885, first published 1851), p. 179.
2. This is evident from accounts provided by white men
brought up by Indians: see, for an example, Edward James, ed.,
*A Narrative of the Captivity and Adventures of John Tanner during
Thirty Years Residence among the Indians in the Interior of North
America* (Minneapolis: Ross and Haines, 1956, first published
1830), pp. 144–147, 168–170, 179–180, 185–186.

leader, however, that religious power came quickly to be ascribed to him. Thus William McLeod wrote misleadingly, that he was an hereditary chief of the Ottawas, and "also a principal priest of the great religious secret society of the Algonkian tribes," [3] which appears to lack all basis in fact.

The story of Pontiac may be quickly told. He was an Ottawa, perhaps a half-breed who had led his own villagers on the side of the French in the American skirmishes between English and French in the period of the War of the Austrian Succession, in the 1740s, and in subsequent battles for the various frontier forts in the 1750s. His fame in Britain grew from the story of his "standing in the path" of Major Robert Rogers who, in 1760, was leading a force to Detroit to receive the surrender of the French garrison, although this story may be untrue.[4] What is better founded in fact, from contemporary sources, is his role in the alliance of tribes which sought to recapture the forts for the French in 1763.

The Indian tribes of the area were largely disaffected under British rule. Their discontents included the shortage of rum and powder (deliberate British policy); the social distance generally maintained by the British (in contrast to the camaraderie of the French); and, in areas further east, (particularly among the Senecas) the gradual encroachment of settlers. There were, of

---

3. William Christie McLeod, *The American Indian Frontier* (New York: Knopf, 1928), p. 407.

4. According to Howard H. Peckham, *Pontiac and the Indian Uprising* (Princeton University Press, 1947), pp. 59–62. This is the most carefully documented work and I have relied upon it.

course, more general disruptive circumstances, including demoralization induced through liquor and disease. The red wampum belt of war had already been sent by the Senecas to several other tribes in 1762, thus the idea of a concerted effort was already in the air before Pontiac plotted his attack on Fort Detroit on April 27, 1763. He may have been stimulated by the hostility of the Senecas to the British, but the particular source of inspiration that he claimed was the message of the Delaware prophet.

The teachings of the prophet were well known in Pennsylvania, and were described by two contemporaries in 1762. The message concerned man in his state of probation on earth and was taught from a leather skin on which there were hieroglyphics representing man's route from earth to heaven. Whereas the ancestors had gone straight to heaven, now men were so immersed in sin that they could not do this: the white man stood across the path. A series of strokes on the parchment represented the sins which the Indians had learned from the whites. The Indians had to learn to live without trade or any intercourse with white people. They must support themselves as their forefathers had done. The use of emetics and abstinence from carnal knowledge were the means to purification. Indians were also to abjure the use of firearms. All these teachings the prophet claimed to have learned in a vision in which he had been shown the path to heaven by a guide sent by the Master of Life. Excessive drinking, fighting each other, taking more than one wife, wardances (in which Indians contacted only an evil spirit) were among the taboos he enjoined. "It was said," wrote John McCullough, who had been a captive of the Delawares, "that their prophet taught them, or made them believe, that he had his instructions immediately from Keesh-she-la-mil-lang-up, or a being that thought us into being, and that by following his instructions, they should in a few years be able to drive white people out of their country." [5] Another version of the prophecy held that there would be three conferences and then war. [6]

The prophet's message was invoked by Pontiac at the council of tribes that he called in late April 1763. But whereas the prophet's message had been to expel all white men, Pontiac's version included a distinction in favour of the French: "I do not forbid you to permit the children of your Father [the French] I love them. They know me and pray to me, and I supply them with their wants and all they give you. But as to those who come to trouble your lands—drive them out, make war upon them. I do not like them at all; they know me not and are my enemies, and the enemies of your brothers." In his version, too, there is an injunction to "drive off your lands those dogs clothed in red. . .". [7]

Pontiac and the prophet did not act in concert, but the prophet's message was invoked by Pontiac for the war he wanted to begin. Nor did Pontiac, as far as is

5. Cited in *ibid.*, p. 99.
6. From the diary of James Kenny, a Pittsburgh Quaker, cited in *ibid.*, pp. 99–100.
7. Milo Milton Quaife, ed., *The Siege of Detroit* (Chicago: The Lakeside Press, 1958), pp. 7–8: the work provides a translation of a contemporary French account, *Journal Dictation d'une Conspiration,* probably written by Robert Navarre.

known, claim to be the anointed war leader. He merely relayed and enlarged the prophetic call to arms. The siege of Detroit itself might not have established Pontiac's reputation, but the fall within a very short space of time, of several other forts, attacked either at Pontiac's behest or by his allies, served to provide one of the vital confirmations of charismatic leadership—success. This alone stimulated cooperation among the jealous Indian tribes, and it is perhaps the case that Pontiac could not so much command war as stimulate it. Certainly he could not maintain a unified command of all the local, fragmented, and volatile bands over a vast territory that today comprises several states: conditions for such unified action simply did not exist. The will to believe the prophet's message was clearly strong, but what the Indians wanted was an immediate transformation of the situation, and, failing such a miracle, charismatic power was both brittle and ephemeral.

The opinions of his enemies may have unduly inflated Pontiac's reputation. Thus one wrote, "The besiegers are led on by an interprising [sic] fellow called Pondiac. He is a genius, for he possesses great bravery, art, and tho' a Catawba prisoner [which was not the case] has had the address to get himself not only at the head of his conquerors, but elected generalissimo of all the confederate forces now acting against us. Perhaps he may deserve to be called the Methridates [sic] of the West." [8] But not all contemporary opinion was exaggerated. One of the Indian agents, George Croghan,

8. Peckham, *Pontiac and the Indian Uprising,* p. 109*n.*

deputy to Sir William Johnson, wrote of him, after the siege had been lifted and Pontiac had accepted a peace settlement with the British, "Pontiac is a shrewd, sensible Indian of few words, and commands more respect amongst these nations than any Indian I ever saw could do amongst his own tribe" (the nations in question were the Illinois tribes, whose territories were a long way west of Detroit).[9] The head of one British delegation to the West, Lt. Alexander Fraser, said of him, "He is in a manner adored by all the nations hereabouts, and he is more remarkable for his integrity and humanity than either Frenchman or Indian in the colony. He has always been as careful of the lives of my men as well as my own as if he had been our father."[10]

Nor was Pontiac himself entirely lacking in claims to leadership. At the conference with Johnson at Fort Ontario, he declared, "I speak in the name of all nations to the westward whom I command," and later, "Father, though you address me, yet it is the same as if you address all the nations."[11] On several occasions he demonstrated his ability to command men of other tribes to do things that were against their inclinations. Perhaps most important of all, he had, during the siege of Detroit, in seeking to rally his forces, specifically made a claim to supernatural knowledge, when speaking to the French *habitants* who lived outside the fort itself. "I know Fort Presqu'Isle has fallen. I say I know it, and this year all the English in Canada, no matter how large their force, must perish. It is the

9. *Ibid.,* p. 282.
10. *Ibid.,* p. 276.
11. *Ibid.,* p. 292.

Master of Life who commands it; He has made known His will unto us, we have responded, and must carry out what He has said, and you French, who know Him better than we, will you all go against His will?" [12]

Although Pontiac lost effective control even of his own Ottawas, and their allied Potawatomies, Chippewas, and Hurons, within the course of a few months, and even though besieged Detroit never fell, Pontiac emerges as one of the first figures, of whom we have direct knowledge among preliterate peoples, who may be said to be charismatic, in that, to legitimate his commands, he invoked the supernatural and took upon himself with some success areas of authority with which he was never formally invested. Momentarily he appeared as if he might draw previously mutually hostile tribes into a common cause—unpropitious as their economic conditions, their level of communications, and their degree of conscious social organization were for such an outcome. That he was a man of exceptional abilities was widely attested at the time (although British officers and agents may have wished to magnify the personal capabilities of an enemy who had some success against them, whether they wrote as Fraser did, or of "a savage of the most refined cunning and treachery natural to the Indians" as General Gage did). Yet it is not his actual abilities that are at issue, so much as his effective claim, using the prophecy of another, to supernatural warrant for the role he assumed. He became, in the course of a very short time, a legend among Indians, and, perhaps more effectively and enduringly a legend among his enemies.

12. *Ibid.*, p. 191.

Tecumseh and Tenskwatawa

The general conditions from which Tecumseh, and his brother, the Shawnee prophet, Laulewasikaw, (who called himself Tenskwatawa—"The Open Door"—on taking up his prophetic role in 1805) emerged were not dissimilar to those against which Pontiac and the Delaware prophet had arisen some four decades earlier. White settlement had advanced, and the Indians had been pushed westwards, so that the Delawares and Shawnees were by this time settled in Indiana territory, which forty years earlier had been the location of the Miamis. The dissipation of Indian culture, in the intermittent warfare with whites (as well as with other tribes) and most especially through the influence of alcohol and firearms, had continued. The Shawnees had suffered further from their alliance with the British in the American revolutionary war, and by the end of the century they, and other tribes lived in brooding discontent. The American government appears to have been eager to push settlement further west and to appropriate Indian lands, and of this the Indians had clear intimation from the broken treaties and steady encroachment that had previously occurred.

The only prospect of remedy for a preliterate people in a situation of this kind is essentially supernatural, and the supernatural itself must be mediated by an agent. Since there are neither resources, nor organizational skills; and since even the perception of the situation is limited, only the miraculous suffices to alter things. This is, of course, a wish-dream, and such a wish is given expression of by a man who voices the longings of a people. In societies dependent on personal trust, the longing for supernatural intervention must be expressed through a man, a man who claims the power to achieve what is desired.

Yet such prophecy also demands action: what is to come will come only if men behave in specific ways. Part of the action is symbolic and part is instrumental. Thus there are divinely prescribed expressive actions, and taboos; and there are more purposive procedures. The former are an earnest of faith, a means of mobilizing men's sentiments and eliciting commitment. The latter are the best-advised steps that can be humanly taken in the circumstances: their success is divinely guaranteed.

As with Pontiac and the Delaware prophet, a division of role occurred between the warrior and the prophet in this case, too. One man sets himself apart and becomes the mouthpiece for the divine, prescribing the ritualistic and expressive activities that are necessary. The other undertakes the human organization. Both must be credible in their roles, and among Indian tribes the shamanistic and prophetic roles were in any case differentiated from the role of the warrior. In the case of Tecumseh and his brother, the division of labour occurs between brothers.

Tecumseh himself had already made a reputation as an orator in conferences with the whites, and had also acquired a reputation as a warrior whilst away in the south where he was well known among the Cherokees. But it was with the succession of his brother, Laulewasikaw, to the role of shaman-prophet, and his adoption of his new name, Tenskwatawa, that charisma may be said to have entered this situation. Tecumseh's existing claim to leadership was now reinforced and elevated by the prophecies of his brother, without which the conscious attempt to build an alliance of tribes across the continent to impede the settlers' advance and—by supernatural aid—to restore the land fully to the Indians, would never have been made.

The prophecies with which Tenskwatawa endorsed his brother's leadership did not, of course, find their origin in his mind. They were now part of a generalized Indian culture. The Shawnees, related to the Delawares, no doubt remembered the teachings of the Delaware prophet of the early 1760s. One Shawnee chief had declared at a convention at Fort Wayne in 1803, before Tenskwatawa emerged as a prophet, that the knowledge which white men possessed had belonged originally to the Shawnees, who had lost it only when they had become corrupt. Further, the whites who took Indian lands, gave goods for it which were ". . . more the property of the Indians than the white people because the knowledge which enabled them to manufacture these goods actually belonged to the Shawnees. . .". But such things would, declared the chief, soon have an end, "The Master of Life is about to restore to the Shawanoes both their knowledge and their rights, and he will trample the long knives under his feet." [13] Thus Tenskwatawa took up a theme

13. This account is given in Benjamin Drake, *The Life of Tecumseh and of his Brother the Prophet, with a historical Sketch of the Shawanoe Indians* (Cincinnati: Rulison, and Philadelphia: Quaker City Publishing House, 1856), pp. 21–22. I have relied principally on this source.

which already had lively currency among his own tribe—and perhaps this is often the case with charismatic leaders. He gave it renewed plausibility, and elaborated it with injunctions, taboos, the story of his own heavenly quest and meeting with the Master of Life, and with a programme of action under his brother which gave these prophecies new vigour and urgency.

Tecumseh himself enjoyed a reputation bordering on the charismatic by virtue of the exaggeration of undoubtedly very considerable personal qualities, but it was the explicit transcendental claims of his brother which make their leadership fully charismatic in the restricted sense in which the term is being deployed in this essay. His military skill, bravery, and nobility of mind were already attested long before his brother assumed the prophetic role. Thus in an account of an engagement between Kentuckian settlers under Simon Kenton and a band of Indians in March 1792, a member of the party, McDonald, recounted,

> The celebrated Tecumseh commanded the Indians. His cautious and fearless intrepidity made him a host wherever he went. In military tactics, night attacks are not allowable, except in cases like this, when the assailing party are far inferior in numbers. Sometimes in night attacks, panics and confusion are created in the attacked party, which may render them a prey to inferior numbers. Kenton trusted to something like this on the present occasion, but was disappointed; for when Tecumseh was present, his influence over the minds of his followers infused that confidence in his tact and intrepidity that they could only be defeated by force of numbers.

In the same affair a white prisoner, McIntire, was taken prisoner by the Indians, and subsequently, in Tecumseh's absence, was killed.

At this act of cruelty to a prisoner, he was exceedingly indignant; declaring that it was a cowardly act to kill a man when tied and a prisoner. The conduct of Tecumseh in this engagement, and in the events of the following morning is creditable alike to his courage and humanity. Resolutely brave in battle, his arm was never lifted against a prisoner, nor did he suffer violence to be inflicted upon a captive, without promptly rebuking it.[14]

Nor was his reputation based merely on military skill and humanity. Following some murders on the frontier in April 1803, white settlers from Chillicothe arranged a conference between the Indians and Governor Tiffin. Colonel John M'Donald reported,

Governor Tiffin opened the conference. "When Tecumseh rose to speak," says an eyewitness, "as he cast his gaze over the vast multitude, which the interesting occasion had drawn together, he appeared one of the most dignified men I ever beheld. While this orator of nature was speaking, the vast crowd preserved the most profound silence. From the confident manner in which he spoke of the intention of the Indians to adhere to the treaty of Greenville, and live in peace and friendship with their white brethren, he dispelled, as if by magic, their apprehensions. . . . The settlers returned to their deserted farms, and business generally was resumed throughout the region." [15]

On all the evidence, Tecumseh was a plausible candidate as a cultural hero, lacking only the legitimation of divine sanction to be accorded that role. For although the various bodies of Indians had certainly attained a considerable degree of intertribal communication in the face of white settlement, and were

14. *Ibid.*, pp. 72–77.   15. *Ibid.*, p. 85.

capable—at least ephemerally and spasmodically—of making common cause with each other, they lacked the economic basis for more permanent military coalescence, and suffered acute local rivalries, fissiparous tendencies, and individual jealousies. Leadership was a precarious role even within a given tribe, and although reputation might go before a man, this was scarcely an adequate basis on which to presume to issue effective commands to people other than his own. Charisma, then, had a relatively unpropitious cultural climate in which to develop.

Tenskwatawa's assumption of the prophetic role was not initially the basis for Tecumseh's claims to supratribal leadership. Tenskwatawa's early injunctions were largely concerned with purification of native life. He condemned drunkenness, acknowledging that he himself was a reformed drunkard; he opposed all innovations in dress and habit; demanded that the young respect the aged; he forbade Indians to take more than one wife in the future, and in particular condemned intermarriage with whites; and he told Indians not to run after women. All medicine bags were to be given up, and their contents destroyed in the presence of the whole community. Instead, Indians were to confess all their faults to the Great Spirit and to beg forgiveness. Despite these commands, which reveal a clear debt to Christian ideas in some respects, there was a strong restorative element in Tenskwatawa's injunctions, too. They were to give up all dogs not of their own breeds, and to give their cats back to the whites. Indians were not to eat food cooked by whites or to use provisions raised by whites, such as bread, pork, or fowls, nor

were they to sell provisions to the whites. Indians
should not offer skins for sale, but must ask for exchange of goods. They were to try to do without buy-
ing merchandise, "by which means game would become plenty and then by means of bows and arrows
they could hunt and kill game as in former days, and
live independent of all white people." [16] More than
anything else, he condemned witchcraft, and some individuals were put to death as witches among the Delawares, which drew a remonstrance from Governor
William Henry Harrison of Indiana, who said that if
Tenskwatawa was a prophet, then the Indians should
ask him to make the sun stand still, the moon alter its
course, the rivers cease to flow, or the dead to rise from
the graves.

The prophet's reputation extended over wide areas,
particularly after he had successfully prophesied an
eclipse of the sun. Indians were invited to "shake
hands with the prophet" by drawing across their hands
four strings of beads, which were supposedly the flesh

16. The items were listed in a letter from Thomas Forsyth to
General William Clark, St. Louis, December 23, 1812, cited by
Emma Helen Blair, ed., *The Indian Tribes of the Upper Missouri
Valley and Region of the Great Lakes* (Cleveland, Ohio: Arthur H.
Clark Co., 1912), vol. II, pp. 274–277. John Tanner reported
that there were also injunctions not to let the fires go out; not to
steal or lie, or strike a man, woman, or child. He also reported a
promise that if they [the Ojjibwas] were obedient, the Sioux,
should they descend on the Ojjibwas, would be unable to see
them because the Great Spirit would protect them: Edward
James, ed., *A Narrative of the Captivity and Adventures of John Tanner during Thirty Years Residence among the Indians in the Interior of
North America* (Minneapolis: Ross and Haines, 1956, first published 1830), p. 144–145.

of Tenskwatawa, as a promise to obey his moral injunctions. "The influence of the Prophet was very sensibly and painfully felt by the remotest Ojibbeways of whom I had any knowledge," wrote John Tanner, a prisoner who lived with the Ojjibwas for many years, "but it was not the common impression among them that his doctrines had any tendency to unite them in the accomplishment of any human purpose. For two or three years drunkenness was much less frequent than formerly; war was less thought of. . . ." [17] It appears to have been only later, when the situation had changed again, with Indian dissatisfaction about the increasing encroachments of the settlers, that Tenskwatawa's prophecies came to the service of the new military objectives of his brother. Although the prophet claimed that he could heal and could preserve men's lives in battle, these were no more than was appropriate for the typical shaman. It was when a new and enlarged scale of military operations was projected, and a much mightier effort to contain the settlers was envisaged, that the old protective devices also needed to be inflated. The prophet's claims then were to endow his brother's leadership with magic on a far greater scale—to legitimate his projected enterprise with supernatural promise.

Undoubtedly the new faith had, at least for a time, a remarkable effect. Although not all Indians were responsive, even including some Shawnees, and although some Delawares, who had at first obeyed the prophet's commands to burn witches, later turned

17. Cited by Drake, *Life of Tecumseh,* p. 103. See also Edward James, *Captivity and Adventures of John Tanner,* pp. 144–147.

against him, none the less, he gained widespread adherence among the Wyandots, Chippewas, Kickapoos, Potawatomies, Ottawas, and Winnebagos, whose chiefs joined Tecumseh in his representations to Governor Harrison against continued white settlement, while some other tribes, not involved in these negotiations, none the less obeyed the injunctions of the prophet. Between 1803 and 1810, Tecumseh had grown aware of the unchanged intentions of the Americans, and although he may have been encouraged by the British in his growing mistrust of the settlers, there is no doubt that the Americans made their treaties with the Indians in bad faith, and with the conscious intention of revoking them, claiming more land and renegotiating new agreements in the future as occasion demanded.[18] Tecumseh's policy of building a dam of all the tribes across the continent was a sophisticated idea for the mind of a savage—anticipated perhaps by Pontiac, but probably beyond the conception of most Indians at that time, and, in the event, certainly beyond their capabilities.

Only the claim to supernatural aid provided Tecumseh with a plausible case among his fellow indigenes, even though he was undoubtedly aware that only war, or the threat of it, would hold the line he proposed to build against the further expansion westwards of the settlers. In demanding that the United States make treaties not with individual Indians and local chiefs, but with all Indians, Tecumseh had a vision of the

18. John M. Oskison, *Tecumseh and His Times* (New York: Putnam, 1938), suggests that Harrison and the United States Government were anxious to alienate Indian lands, pp. 109, 139.

needs of the natives which far transcended the individ-
ualistic and local preoccupations that characterized Indian life. His mission was necessarily involved in attempting to educate and acclimatize Indians to a new
conception of themselves and their prospects. It was
with this intention that he canvassed his case to tribes
remote from his own, and did so in the strength which
his brother's restorative vision provided.

Charisma is a quality that, once evoked in the affairs
of men, is not easily confined to particular individuals
or occasions. It readily overspills to suffuse entire situations. There is a strong infectiousness in the demand
for magical solutions, and a tendency for the claims to
such power to grow, not only in the subsequent tell-
ing, but in the direct apprehension of the situation by
participants. Evoked by Tenskwatawa, it became also
associated with Tecumseh's own power, instanced by
what is told of his mission to the Creeks in Alabama.
Putting his demand for their aid in his cause, Tecumseh threatened that if it was not forthcoming, he
would return north and go to Detroit, and that once he
was there he would stamp and cause their houses in
Tuckhabatchee to fall. On the day that they calculated
that he might be there, an earthquake did indeed destroy houses in Tuckhabatchee.

Magic is not only infectious, but it is also intoxicat-
ing. The charismatic claims of the prophet were made
with such confidence that he contrived to lead himself
astray by them—perhaps believing implicitly in them.
The premature termination of Tecumseh's policy concerns us only to complete the story. Warriors of
various tribes had assembled at Tippecanoe as Indian

discontent had mounted, and Governor Harrison had summoned a regiment of United States infantry to Vincennes for protection and, in October and November 1811, he deployed his troops to neutralize the threat of the large assembly of Indians. In the absence of Tecumseh, the prophet promised the warriors that they could not be harmed by bullets, and prompted them into a disastrous action against the United States troops. The prophet's own hold over his followers was now broken, and the prospect of a dam of tribes disappeared for ever. In the future the common circumstance of Indian tribes was to induce them to accept each other more readily than in the past, (although until the very end of their independent freedom of action, tribes like the Sioux continued to engage in warfare with their traditional Indian enemies). The alliances which, by claiming prophetic aid, a man like Tecumseh might forge, were not themselves durable. But that they should have arisen at all may be attributed primarily to the charismatic claims made for their designer and his brother. That Tecumseh and Tenskwatawa failed does not impugn the charismatic element in the situation: charisma always fails in the longer run and taken on its own terms, although men may long continue to believe its claims. They can persist, of course, only by being spiritualized and by losing their empirical application: the brevity of the Shawnee vision and the general cultural circumstances of Indians ruled out any such development in this case. The strength of this example lies in the relative success attained: only the charismatic, the claim to superhuman power, was sufficient to draw the Indians together, to surrender some element of local power to promote a pressing common concern. Tecumseh was of course, a worthy vessel for divine grace, and his personal renown undoubtedly added plausibility to the claims made by his brother on behalf of them both. But that this was not the substance of the charismatic appeal is clear from the very different character of his brother, Tenskwatawa, who, after all, really stimulated obedience by his promises. He, on all the evidence, was a man of different mettle, described as vain, loquacious and cunning, and of indolent habits.[19] And yet he could successfully claim divine inspiration, which perhaps makes apparent the irrelevance of personality characteristics for the success of the charismatic claim to power.

William Wadé Harris

Just as particular movements may arise without the inspiration of a charismatic leader, so an individual may come to exercise charismatic power and to command a following without leaving behind him a single well-defined, coherent, and persisting movement. Charisma is a social relationship, but not all men in a given situation readily accord the claim to authority made by, or on behalf of, the would-be charismatic. There are always half-believers, drifters, doubters, and

19. The local Shakers, who met the prophet, whilst not explicitly denying or referring to such judgments, believed the prophet to be a peaceable and good man: John Candee Dean, ed., *Journal of Thomas Dean: A Voyage to Indiana* (Indiana Historical Society Publication VI, 2, 1918), pp. 273–345, p. 308.

sceptics, even in a population in which the claim to charisma is widely accepted. And there are always those who, impressed at one time, are indifferent at another. Some, perhaps, are too well entrenched in established institutional relationships to find it necessary or desirable to acknowledge a new source of power. Some may see the new claim as a threat to existing status systems in which they have a vested interest. Some may be educated beyond the appeal of the charismatic: others may be too little touched by the insecurities of a changing social situation to need new inspirational guidance. Whether a well-articulated movement will come into being once a charismatic figure emerges must also depend on more than his mere social acceptance. In particular, of course, the extent to which a persisting movement arises from his activity will depend on the extent to which a lieutenant arises who is capable of providing regular, institutional procedures and systematic organization. We do not here need to delineate the conditions for institutional persistence: we need only acknowledge that there are many styles of charismatic figure. Prophets and warrior-kings are not all of a kind: nor are their social consequences. And whilst a charismatic warrior normally brings into being an army, a prophet may function without any such coherent following. There may not be one recognizable movement as a consequence of prophetic activity. There may be several, or there may be only collective recollection of his activity. The criterion of charisma is not consequences: a powerful social relationship may come into being and influence men without leading to revolution or even to a new church.

The prophet, William Wadé Harris, accomplished a relatively brief itinerant preaching mission in the Ivory Coast and the western Gold Coast in 1913 to 1914. He left behind him an inchoate and perhaps volatile following loosely known (in the Ivory Coast) as *Harristes,* which subsequently developed into a number of separate movements and churches.[20] That he was a powerful charismatic leader cannot be doubted even though the remaining evidences of his activity differ considerably from the legacy of many other claimants.

Harris was a prophet in the Christian tradition, modelled perhaps on the figures of the Old Testament, but with a simplified message which was easily accepted by indigenes who had often little or no previous acquaintance with Christianity. He firmly believed in his own God-given powers, threatened his listeners with fire from heaven if they disobeyed, and sometimes reduced his listeners to fearful trembling and convulsions. Such was his impact that the French authorities in the Ivory Coast considered that he was a powerful hypnotist. In his relatively short active career in the Ivory Coast and the Gold Coast, his preaching deeply affected many thousands, sometimes transforming the entire way of life of some primitive communities.[21]

Born in Liberia about 1865 to pagan parents of the

20. B. Holas, *Le Separatisme religieux en Afrique noire* (Paris: P.U.F., 1965), and J. F. Köbben, "Prophetic Movements as an Expression of Social Protest," *International Archives of Ethnography* 49, Pt. 1, (1960): 117–164.

21. I have relied principally on Gordon MacKay Haliburton, *The Prophet Harris* (London: Longmans, 1971), which is the most thoroughly documented account.

Grebo tribe, Harris acquired his knowledge of Christianity from a local "minister," who had been converted by the missionaries who had come to the area with the settlement of returned Negroes from the United States. He obtained a knowledge of English from service in British ships that plied the West African coast, and which relied on the Kru tribes (of which the Grebos are one) for labour. It was by adopting the name of the master of one such vessel that he acquired his first and last names.[22] Returning to Liberia, Harris became a teacher for a number of years—a role which, at that time and in that part of the world called for no more than a rudimentary education, and some commitment to Christianity. Harris belonged at this time to the Protestant Episcopal Church, although he was also said to have belonged to a group that claimed to use their knowledge of ancient Egyptian occultism. (A number of spurious occult works circulated on the West Coast of Africa in these years, claiming to provide a knowledge of secret mysteries.) [23] This charge may, however, have been merely an accusation of his enemies, for by this time (1908), Harris was in opposition to the local chief and was becoming identified

22. This is asserted in the essentially popular account of Margaret Musson, *Prophet Harris: the Amazing Story of Old Pa Union Jack* (Wallington: Religious Education Press, 1950), p. 52.

23. Some account of the circulation in West Africa of these works is given in B. Holas, *Le Separatisme religieux,* pp. 220 ff., and in H. W. Turner, "Pagan Features in West African Independent Churches," *Practical Anthropology* 12, 4 (July–August, 1965): 145–151.

with the dissident Kru peoples who opposed the dominance in their area of the American Negro Liberians.

The principal hope of the Krus was to assert their connection with the British, and in 1909 an unruly British Frontier Force in Sierra Leone, and the activities of the British Consul in Liberia led the Liberians to suspect that the British were planning a *coup d'état* in favour of the Kru tribes.[24] Harris identified himself with the pro-British Grebos and according to some accounts he regularly raised the British flag over his house in these years. In 1909 he was involved in an incident in which he was said to have insulted the Liberian flag and to have raised the British flag in its place. Although he may by no means have been plotting rebellion, and may not have been in any sense a leader of a revolutionary group, this incident has sometimes been associated with Harris's subsequent career as a prophet.

During the period of imprisonment to which he was sentenced for his "treasonable" act, Harris felt himself called as a prophet: as Haliburton says, he "experienced the extraordinary physical and mental sensations which for him meant that God had sent His messenger, the Archangel Gabriel, to commission him as a prophet." [25] In 1912, Harris was released from prison, and in a new garb consisting of a loose white sheet, a turban, and carrying a cross about six feet in height, made of bamboo, he now started his preaching career. At this stage, Harris, who was said to have spoken "excellent English," claimed to have had no education,

24. G. M. Haliburton, *The Prophet Harris,* pp. 26–32.
25. *Ibid.,* p. 35.

and said that his English was the gift of the Spirit, together with his knowledge of the Bible.[26]

The Ivory Coast, whence Harris went, was at this time relatively little influenced by the Roman Catholic missionaries whom the French authorities had allowed to work there, and the interior of the country had been effectively brought under control only two or three years before Harris's itinerary. His reputation was acquired quickly and soon preceded him. He was accepted as a new god. Everywhere stories circulated of his remarkable power, particularly his power to detect hidden fetiches and to destroy them. He was reputed to be able to curse those who opposed him and to cause their sudden death or instant blindness. He acquired a reputation as a rainmaker (and when interviewed in later life, asserted this claim himself). On the model of Elijah, he is supposed to have confronted local sorcerers who threatened him with sudden illness: their failure enhanced Harris's reputation still further. Those who once accepted conversion and then reneged were said to fall victim to Harris's power and were struck down with disease or death. Administrators and missionaries who stood in his way were also reputed to have been suddenly afflicted in the days following a confrontation with him.[27]

These popular impressions of his power were echoed in the accounts by observers. J. H. Casely Hayford, a

26. *Ibid.,* p. 37; J. G. Casely Hayford (Ekra-Agyiman), *William Waddy Harris, The West African Reformer: The Man and his Message* (London: C. M. Phillips, 1915), p. 8, wrote, "Harris is a Kroo man of low birth and no education. In his own words: 'I know no book'."

27. G. M. Haliburton, *The Prophet Harris,* pp. 70, 77.

barrister-at-law in Axim, Gold Coast, wrote enthusi-
astically in his praise, and recounted with only
guarded incredulity, one widely reported testimony to
Harris's power. "He is strong against Sabbath-break-
ing, and he makes men realise what he means. With
outstretched hand towards the sea he points to the
boats working on the Lord's day, and hints at strange
things that are about to happen. A ship in the neigh-
bourhood takes fire the same day. There is nothing
strange in that. It is a mere accident. It can be explained away. So can a good many things. All the
same, it is a curious coincidence." [28] Investigating
Harris's activities some eight or nine years later, Platt
discovered belief in the same event, "He had set fire to
a steamer . . . [which] was unloading cargo on the
Sabbath. He had walked upon the water. . . ." [29]

Nor is there any doubt about the effect that Harris
had on his listeners. Captain Paul Marty, a French
government official described his activities:

> Le procédé de conversion du "Prophète" est toujours le
> même; il se rend dans un village, la foule se réunit autour
> de lui, les hommes à sa droite et les femmes à sa gauche.
> Il leur clame alors d'une voix tonitruante tout le mal que
> leur font les fétiches et ordonne aux sorciers de venir se
> placer devant lui. Il leur montre sa croix. Ceux-ci sont
> alors pris de convulsions, cherchent à fuir, mais ne le
> peuvent, se roulent en hurlant. Ils paraissent à ce mo-
> ment en état hypnotique. Harris les calme et leur trace
> sur le front un signe de croix avec de l'eau en leur faisant
> tenir sa croix. Les sorciers vont alors d'eux-mêmes briser
> leurs idoles. Le village se fait baptiser.

28. J. G. Casely Hayford, *William Waddy Harris,* p. 8.
29. W. J. Platt, *An African Prophet* (London, SCM Press,
1934), p. 32.

Le bruit se répandit peu a peu que ceux qui n'obéis-
saient point à ses conseils moraux en étaient aussitôt
punis, non par la mort que donnaient les fétiches, mais
par l'empêchement de commettre la mauvaise action
qu'ils se proposaient d'accomplir.[30]

The effects were described by an Englishman who had
been at Fresco when the prophet arrived. He told
Platt, "Folks . . . were sunk in debased superstition
and fetish-worship, and had been so for years. In three
days this prophet fellow—I heard him preach myself—
changed all that. Their fetihes were burnt and what
was an ordinary African coast village, steeped in superstition, became nominally a Christian town." [31]

Harris stuck to a coastal route both in his journey
through the Ivory Coast to Apollonia (the Nzima tribal
area of the western Gold Coast) and on his return. His
emissaries were sent to mission in the interior. Many of
these were Fanti clerks who had been converted before,
and their reliability was, of course, variable. Some of
them became extortioners, using the opportunity of
religious excitement to make money: but this is a phenomenon commonly found in the wake of new religious enthusiasms. Beyond their influence, news of
the new prophet extended further inland. The Attiés at
Akoupe believed that the great god of the sky had de-
scended to destroy fetiches, and others believed that if
they obeyed the new injunctions to destroy fetiches
and build churches they would thereafter be exempted
from the payment of taxes.[32] Such demands are com-

---

30. Paul Marty, *Études sur l'Islam en Côte d'Ivoire* (Paris: Édi-
tions Ernest Leroux, 1922), p. 15.

31. W. J. Platt, *An African Prophet,* p. 34.

32. G. M. Haliburton, *The Prophet Harris,* pp. 124–125.

monly attached to prophetic activities, since men seek a world in which their particular burdens are removed. *Harrisme* was thus many sided, and part of its appeal undoubtedly came from the idea that soon by its agencies the French colonial authorities would go away, or at least that by acceptance of it they would increase their power against the colonial authorities. Whilst most Harris converts were induced to accept baptism and join one or other Christian church, or to form one, some of the interior tribes understood neither the specifically Christian character of the movement nor implemented the demands for an orderly Christian way of life.

Harris's preaching was simple and dramatic. He taught only a few central ideas. Fetiches were to be destroyed; men were to love God and their neighbours; theft, false witness, and covetousness were forbidden; men had to work, resting on Sundays; monogamy was recommended, but polygamy was not forbidden, and Harris himself may have had relations with several different women followers. He demanded confession of sins, and provided immediate baptism without any previous instruction, maintaining that baptism itself would give people the power to change. He used both the cross and the Bible to dispel fear and cast out evil and disease. Although he denied that they had intrinsic power, and readily had another one made if his cross was broken,[33] there can be little doubt that many who accepted the prophet regarded both cross and Bible as objects of superior magical quality.

33. Katesa Schlosser, *Propheten in Afrika* (Braunschweig: Albert Limbach Verlag, 1949), p. 255.

Undoubtedly, Harris may be seen primarily as the instigator of an anti-witchcraft movement not dissimilar from others found in widely separated parts of Africa—Kimbangu in the Congo, Alice Lenshina in Zambia, and the well-documented earlier witchcraft eradication movements of the Rhodesias. Even in the Ivory Coast, in many areas his was by no means the first impulse toward the elimination of fetiches, although his movement was, for many indigenes, the first that sought to destroy fetiches in the name of Christianity, and which did so without the economic extortion of earlier cults. His success thus rested on the strong sense of his "power," and although he did not remain in the Ivory Coast for very long (he was deported at the end of 1914, and was not allowed to return) and his leadership was never institutionalized among the people who obeyed his commands, nonetheless he can be regarded as very much a charismatic leader.

His own claims in this respect continued in later life. He was visited by various missionaries, and was known to others in Liberia where he continued to preach, until his death in 1929, though never with the same success as in the Ivory Coast. He had a considerable if brief success in Sierra Leone, where he was regarded as a powerful healer. But his self-estimation was never in doubt. He claimed that his prophetic robes had been given to him by the Archangel Gabriel, who had accompanied him on his journeys. He received—so he said—telegrams from heaven. The gift of tongues, he claimed, had enabled him to preach in French. He told Fr. Peter Harrington, S.M.A., that he "was one of the twelve apostles commissioned by God to work in the modern world. Four of these were assigned to Africa, Harris having West Africa as his charge. He was [at the time of the interview] on his way north to Sierra Leone to meet with his colleague of the north. When the great blood-letting was finished in Europe, they would meet there to dictate to the rulers of the earth the conditions in which the rule of Christ on earth, the millennium, would begin." [34]

It is evident, that both in respect of his self-claims, and in the effect that he had on the lives of thousands of followers in the Ivory Coast and western Ghana, that Harris must be ranked as a charismatic leader. The churches that were built in response to his commands, and the complete transformation of the way of life of some natives stand as testimonies to his effectiveness. The Provincial Commissioner of the western province of the Gold Coast wrote, "Apollonia before Harris [sic] visit was steeped in fetishism and the towns and villages were in a most unsanitary condition. All that has now been changed, places of worship and schools are to be found in every village, and the villages and towns are being remodelled on sanitary lines." [35]

Some of the changes which Harris persuaded the natives to undertake had, of course, been canvassed earlier by the administration. The French in the Ivory Coast had in particular seen the *féticheurs* as the principal opponents to their policy, as the instigators of revolt as well as being the leaders of resistance to the changes they wished to implement. But it was Harris

34. G. M. Haliburton, *The Prophet Harris,* p. 190.
35. Quoted by G. M. Haliburton, *ibid.,* p. 90.

rather than the French who succeeded in countering the power of the *féticheurs* and in getting the fetiches themselves destroyed. Nor, despite the brevity of his mission, were the effects temporary. Nine or ten years later, when Platt succeeded in getting French permission to take Methodist missionaries into the Ivory Coast, the churches were still functioning even if, in some cases, the local administrators had actually burned the buildings. He found in each meeting place a copy of an English Family Bible on a desk or a table, honoured but unread, apparently regarded as something almost magical.[36] Harris himself, and his promise that others would come to teach the Bible were still remembered, and provided the basis for the Methodist work in that part of Africa. The twelve leaders that he usually appointed in each village had remained faithful to the idea, even if their actual knowledge of Christianity was slight (for Harris apparently taught little about Christ as such, but concentrated on the ten commandments, and a few simple moral rules to replace the power of the *féticheurs* whom he displaced). In the western Gold Coast, the Harris followers organized themselves into one of the first independent churches in what is to-day Ghana, taking the same leadership principle as their title, *The Church of the Twelve Apostles*. The foundress, Grace Thannie, an illiterate woman and former fetich priestess, was one of those who had been most closely associated with Harris during his itinerant mission.[37]

36. W. J. Platt, *An African Prophet,* pp. 35, 71.

37. On this movement, see C. G. Baëta, *Prophetism in Ghana* (London: SCM Press, 1962), pp. 9–27.

Simon Kimbangu

It is implicit in the sociological concept of charisma that the myth is always bigger—immeasurably bigger—than the man. Since the sociologist is necessarily, to borrow Peter Berger's term, methodologically agnostic, he must always deny the claim of divine inspiration even though he may emphasize the importance of the fact that such a claim is made and recognizes that in being made, such a claim may become the basis for important new forms of social relationship which may radically affect the course of social events. In the case of Simon Kimbangu the disparity of the myth and the man is perhaps greater than in most cases, for the period between Kimbangu's sudden renown as a healer and his trial and lifelong imprisonment was brief. In that period of seven months a sufficient corpus of legend had accumulated to establish his name as that of a unique spiritual saviour of his people and to inspire over several succeeding decades a wide range of imitators, whose diverse aims were politically or spiritually often quite different from his own. His acclaim was such that his name eventually came to provide the basis for a national Congolese religious movement that has been steadily institutionalized into a new independent African church. Such indeed was the abundance and the extravagance of the myths surrounding the name of Kimbangu that in order to make the principal religious organization that arose in his name, *L'Église de Jésus Christ sur la Terre par le Prophète Simon Kimbangu,* acceptable to Christians generally, and to the World Council of Churches in particular, a considerable process of demythologization had to occur.

Our concern, however, is precisely with the significance of myth. For whatever construction is now put on the stories about Kimbangu's life and experiences, there can be little doubt that without those stories Kimbangu would not have acquired the following that he did. The simple Congolese tribesmen had heard a good deal about Christianity: it was the emergence of a prophet of their own, about whom incredible things were told, that brought a movement into being, that caused thousands to abandon their work and flock to his village of Nkamba. It was not to hear repeated the stories of Christ, told less well perhaps by a catechist than by the more experienced missionaries, but to acclaim a saviour of their own, and to see and experience the miracles that he was said continually to perform. It is now claimed that Kimbangu was essentially a simple Christian, those faith was—it is conceded even by his strongest Christian defenders—somewhat coloured by the cultural conditions in which he grew up. That may have been the case. But there can be no doubt that it was precisely the less than orthodox aspects of his ministry—the instantaneous healings, the ecstatic speaking in tongues, the witch-cleansing, and the stories of miracles—which most attracted his vast following. The martyrdom conferred on him by the Belgian authorities, and his own elaborate imitation of the final episodes before the arrest of Christ, undoubtedly added to his appeal.

Simon Kimbangu was probably a better educated man than William Wadé Harris, and aspired, after being educated in the Baptist Mission near his home village, to become a pastor of that church.[38] The formal requirements for such a role at that time (just after the First World War) were not by modern standards exacting. The missions—in accordance with their old shibboleth, and to meet the growing costs of the hopeless missionary task with which they were faced—were more and more hoping to produce self-sufficient and self-recruiting churches, and to that end mission education was promoted in order to produce, as quickly as conditions and the very constrained cultural background of candidates would allow, an army of local pastors. Kimbangu did not, however, pass the examinations that would have allowed him to take up pastoral work, and he was therefore destined to remain a mere catechist. Not unlike others before him (Ositelu in Nigeria, founder of the Aladura Church of the Lord, and Hung Hsiu-Chüan in China, who inspired the T'ai-p'ing rebellion are comparable cases) Kimbangu's failure in examinations, prompted him to seek a swifter route to high social status. Like Ositelu he began to have visions, and, like him, found himself called to a higher work than the one to which men's examination systems could assign him.[39]

38. He is said to have, ". . . attended a mission village school long enough to have become semiliterate and to have acquired baptism" by James E. Bertsche, "Kimbangu: A Challenge to Missionary Statesmanship," *Practical Anthropology* 13 (January–February, 1966): 13–33.

39. Particular importance is attached to this examination failure by Georges Balandier, "Messianism and Nationalism in Black Africa," in Pierre L. van den Berghe, *Africa: Social Problems of Change and Conflict* (San Francisco: Chandler, 1965), pp. 443–460, 449. On Ositelu, see H. W. Turner, *African Independent Church* (Oxford: Clarendon Press, 1967).

Although claiming not to have heeded the first visions (and this is again not unusual, as biblical precedents suggest), Kimbangu came to believe that he had been distinctly endowed by the grace of God. He claimed to heal the sick, restore the dead to life, and overcome the power of fetiches. According to Balandier, he spoke of himself as the Messenger of God and the Son of God, "attempting in this way to associate himself with the symbol of the Trinity, and he took the name *Gounza* (which in the Ki-Kongo language means 'all these at once'). The word is also the Ki-Kongo equivalent of Messiah. . . ." [40] The tradition, despite the reinterpretation of Kimbanguism by various white commentators, still persists. "His name is often pronounced and he is sometimes bracketed together in a surprising and vague manner with the third person of the Trinity; his aid is often invoked." [41] There is, thus, no doubt of the charismatic claim of Kimbangu, nor of the persisting belief in it, even as expressed in directly Christian terms.

Kimbangu's brief career after his call was not untypical of the prophetic leader in the Christian tradition. Beginning to preach independently, he soon earned a reputation as a healer, and perhaps more specifically as a powerful destroyer of fetiches, *minkisi.* The evidence suggests that at this stage his preaching did not differ significantly from that of the Protestant missionaries from whom he had acquired what he knew of scripture. At first their missions were filled by

40. G. Balandier, *The Sociology of Black Africa,* trans. Douglas Garman (London: Deutsch, 1970), p. 415.

41. Jean Lasserre and François Choffat, "Journey in the Congo, *Reconciliation Quarterly* 133, (2nd Quarter, 1966): 666.

Kimbangu's enthusiastic followers, and there was a vigorous demand for Bibles. But very soon, as his reputation spread, and as he built an enclosure outside his own house, it no longer sufficed for men to obtain Kimbangu's message from the missionaries. Although Kimbangu's cures were certainly few—and those not well attested—hospitals were soon deserted. The new prophet began to commission black assistants, and there was a widespread experience of ecstasy. Kimbangu professed to be able to discern spirits in the biblical manner, and this discernment was immediately turned towards the control of witches. Whereas the white missionaries were disposed to reject the idea that witchcraft existed at all, and forbade witchcraft accusations, Africans were convinced of the existence of witches. What they wanted was not the denial of witchcraft but the elimination of witches. By discerning spirits Kimbangu fulfilled a powerfully felt need in Congolese society and may have been all the more capable of doing this since, according to reports, his own father had been a *féticheur*. As in other anti-witchcraft movements, the idea developed that no witch could approach the powerful spirit embodied in the new prophet. Those who came from a distance to see Kimbangu would die if they were witches: any deaths that occurred were of course simultaneously evidence of his power and proof of the theory. Fetiches were destroyed and there is some evidence that baptism was used as a protection against witchcraft.[42]

Extra trains were needed for pilgrims who wanted to

42. J. van Wing, "Le Kimbanguisme vu par un témoin," *Zaïre (Revue Congolese)* XII, 6, (1958): 563–618, 575.

be healed by the new saviour, but the mass pilgrimages quickly aroused the anxiety of officials. The ecstasy, speaking in tongues, and the extensive excitement all appeared as threats to civic order. Kimbangu does not appear to have been particularly anti-white, but the government reaction to his movement undoubtedly precipitated its development in that direction.[43] His first encounter with Morel, the District Commissioner, apparently provided some indication of Kimbangu's disdain for authority, but in seeking his arrest, destroying his village, subjecting him to a trial in which the elementary rules of justice were completely ignored, and in sentencing him to death (later commuted to life imprisonment), the authorities indicated the extent of their own hostility to independent religious movements which they feared as expressions of pan-Africanism, if not as political movements. In all, Kimbangu was active for no more than six months—from mid-March to mid-September 1921 —and for half of this time he was a fugitive. He was arrested in September tried in October and by November he had been deported to Katanga where he was to spend the remaining thirty years of his life.

Even in this short time, however, his impact had been considerable. Roman Catholic missions had been very much affected by the new movement, and although the Protestant missionaries had been not unfriendly, and condemned the severity of the sentence

43. I have chiefly followed the detailed account by Efraim Andersson, *Messianic Popular Movements in the Lower Congo* (Studia Ethnographica Upsaliensia, XIV, Stockholm: Almqvist and Wicksell, 1958).

on Kimbangu, they too had doubts about the extent to which the movement focussed on the blackness of the prophet, and the extent of his messianic claims. More important, however, was the accumulation of myth around the name of the messiah. He was credited with many healings, though in the nature of the case and the circumstances prevailing, these remain unauthenticated. He is said to have had a vision to go and heal a child; he is reputed—after the manner of Jesus—to have healed a woman and ordered the local evangelist to see the miracle. He is reputed to have restored life to a dead child, only to see it die again because of the mother's lack of faith, and later to have resuscitated a seven-year-old child. He is said to have healed a blind man by making mud from his own spittle with which the blind man's eyes were bathed.[44]

The modern reader will doubt the authenticity of these stories, although a considered attempt has been made to suggest their validity—and their conformity to the best orthodox Christian tradition by writers who have sought to absolve Kimbangu from the accusations of engaging in traditional healing practices and of holding syncretistic beliefs. One writes, "If he incorporated other primitive beliefs in his doctrine it was not from policy, but because they formed a part of his own cultural heritage. In the domain of ritual he was strongly influenced by traditional pre-Christian concepts, but doctrinally he upheld the pure tenets of

44. These accounts are given in Marie-Louise Martin, *Kirche Ohne Weisse* (Basel: Friedrich Reinhardt Verlag, 1971), pp. 71–74.

Christianity." [45] Others have gone rather further, ignoring Balandier's assertion that Kimbangu strongly supported the ancestor cult, and have attempted to draw a sharp distinction between the traditional practices of healing and the stories of Kimbangu's miracles, crediting all non-Christian practice to the "false prophets," *Bangunza,* who appeared in considerable numbers in the period of Kimbangu's six months of prophetic activity. [46]

Fortunately, we need not attempt to assess the authenticity of these stories. Undoubtedly, Kimbangu modelled himself on Jesus, both in his practice and in the manner in which he surrendered himself to the authorities and conducted himself at his trial. [47] Whether this is taken as a proof of his Christianity or as a blasphemy is beside the point of our discussion. Nor need we decide whether his success was primarily a Christian revival or a precursor of political awakening under a religious veneer: it seems improbable that these elements can be adequately disentangled even though the evidence for any conscious political orientation appears to be very weak. All that we need note is the powerful charismatic claim and its considerable success. Undoubtedly, even before his imprisonment,

45. Harold W. Fehderau, "Kimbanguism: Prophetic Christianity in the Congo," *Practical Anthropology* 9, (July–August, 1962): 157–178.

46. G. Balandier, *The Sociology of Black Africa,* p. 516; M-L. Martin, *Kirche Ohne Weisse,* pp. 84–85.

47. For an account emphasizing this parallel, see Jules Chomé, *La Passion de Simon Kimbangu, 1921–51,* 2nd ed. (Brussels: Les Amis de "Présence Africaine," 1959).

Kimbangu was a very considerable charismatic figure, capable of summoning widespread faith. And this assertion can be made without regard to the man's own qualities or the orthodoxy of his Christian belief and practice: a highly significant social relationship came into being between this man, or his projected image, and a sizeable section of the Congolese masses.[48] This relationship, this awakening of a vigorous *charismatic demand* continued after his trial and, in his name, inspired a congeries of movements in the Congo, the vigour of which has by no means evaporated more than half a century later.

The concept of charismatic demand is the only one which serves to explain the plethora of prophetism that developed in the Congo in the period between the two world wars. As a concept it focusses our attention less on the man who becomes the charismatic claimant, and more on the social conditions in which men are prepared to demand—through the instrumentality of the exceptional individual, or the individual whom they are prepared to regard as exceptional—a radical change in their social experience, their relationships and the structure of society.

The contemporary Christian apologists of Kimbanguism are obliged to resort frequently to the concept of "false prophets" in order to distinguish the traditional styles of which they approve: the sociologist

48. M-L. Martin, *Kirche Ohne Weisse,* appears to misunderstand the sociological concept of charisma, attributing it directly to Kimbangu's personal appeal, very much as a believer might do, when she writes, e.g., "Er war erstaunlich nuchtern, trotz seines Charisma . . . ," p. 67.

knows no such distinction. Periods of widespread prophetism are themselves likely to be periods of acute social change, with changing economic and political experiences and expectations. The consequences for the Congo of the end of the First World War and the drastic changes that it entailed for the Congolese economy were perhaps sufficient to induce the widespread desire for radical solutions to contemporary problems. Prophetism always entails the wish for dramatic changes to meet contemporary circumstances and to cope with prevailing evils. The prophets may reaffirm traditional solutions, and seek to restore past practices in the lapse of which they seek to trace the cause of prevailing ills. They may espouse the future, the ideas of an imported culture, and act as catalytic agents of modernization and change. Perhaps most frequently they represent a syncretistic posture, setting themselves over against both the actual past and the innovations of the present.

In the wake of Kimbangu, and usually in his name, which had come to symbolize indigenous genius against the oppression of the colonial authorities, large numbers of local prophets arose. Some may indeed have been active before the emergence of Kimbangu, but once his trial had occurred and his healing cult had been prohibited, the name of Kimbangu was the celebrated name by which new prophets asserted their own claims, whether their practice was in the broadly Christian tradition of Kimbangu or not.

Those prophets who emerged after Kimbangu enjoyed an essentially derived charisma by professing to speak in his name. Some were no more than traditional witch-curers. Others were advocates of the traditional

ancestor cult, and some may have been quasi-Christian
catechists. Such was the confusion, that the authorities
demanded that all catechists obtain a license before
embarking on preaching activities. In the 1930s many
local leaders canvassed a distinctly adventist and anti-
white doctrine, whilst others proclaimed visions similar to those of Kimbangu. Forest meetings also occurred in which the more ecstatic elements that had
marked Kimbangu's early practice acquired special importance, including manifestations of "tongues," con-
fessions, and jerks, as well as ordeals by fire, and lech-
erous dancing in an orgiastic atmosphere.[49]

Prophetism spread to the French Congo where,
under André Matswa the more overtly political potential of Kimbanguism was exploited. Matswa had
served in the Moroccan campaigns with the French
army and had lived for a time in Paris, where he
founded a friendly society for his fellow expatriates,
the *Amicale Balali.* He and his agents collected funds
for purposes which remained somewhat obscure even
to the contributors, but an inchoate dream of independence from colonial authorities and repossession of the
land grew up. Such dreams were not dissipated by
Matswa's subsequent arrest, imprisonment and, in
1942, his death. Matswa's politically inspired movement never lacked religious connotations and eventually it proliferated and developed into yet another of
the congeries of cults, in some of which Matswa was
identified with Jesus, and was expected to become

49. E. Andersson, *Messianic Popular Movements,* p. 103; Karl
Aldén, "The Prophet Movement in Congo," *International Review
of Missions* 25 (1936): 347–353.

"king" of the northern bank of the Congo River and the equivalent of Kimbangu in the eyes of the latter's followers in the Belgian Congo.

Just as the political concerns of Matswa's followers became inextricably mixed with atavistic religious practice, so the ambitious *Mission des Noires* of Simon Mpadi welded traditional ritualism, borrowed Salvationist trappings and hierarchy, and ideas of a utopian kingdom to be established on earth. He and Mavonda Ntangu were prominent among the prophet leaders of the *Khakists,* so-called from the uniforms they adopted. Kimbangu was invoked in the prayers they said, and Mpadi claimed to be his mouthpiece. Matswa too was sometimes regarded as a member of the hierarchy. Despite arrest, imprisonment, escape, and exile as a fugitive, Mpadi managed to retain some control over an organization which the authorities considered both formidable and fanatical.[50] Its meetings included a variety of ecstatic (but apparently not orgiastic) practices, including the drinking of water sucked up from graves, as a sign of complete commitment.[51] Ntangu certainly claimed mystical powers, whilst Mpadi, after returning from imprisonment and in the early days of the independence of Zaïre, set himself up as a king over his obligatorily polygamous followers and prescribed elaborate rituals for religious occasions.[52]

50. G. Balandier, *Sociology of Black Africa,* p. 435.

51. *Ibid.,* p. 446; E. Andersson, *Messianic Popular Movements,* pp. 170–175.

52. G. Bernard and P. Caprasse, "Religious Movements in the Congo: A Research Hypothesis," *Cahiers Économiques et Sociaux* (Lovanium, Congo) III, 1, (March 1965): 49–59.

The troubled circumstances which followed the
First World War gave rise to many other prophet
movements in the Congo. National independence in
1958 by no means brought to an end the days of the
prophets. Many of them took Kimbangu as their prototype or professed to speak in his name, but perhaps
more impressive than the line of successors was the
conspicuous and persistent demand for a prophet.
Kimbangu's arrest no doubt gave rise to the demand
for his return, and in a more general way to a demand
for divinely inspired leadership. The educational level
of the indigenes was such that they conceived the solution to their social, economic, and political problems
essentially to be a messiah, a man of superordinate
power who might at a stroke resolve the tensions, frus-
trations, and deprivations of everyday life.

Movements in Search of Leaders

It is by no means contended here that all new religious movements are charismatic movements. Nor is
it necessary in order to rehabilitate the concept, to do
more than show that charisma is *sometimes* the most
powerful element in bringing new movements into
being. But we have already suggested, in looking at
the emergence of prophetism in the Congo that there is
such a thing as charismatic demand. In that case the
demand may have been considerably, if not entirely,
stimulated by the brief and dramatic career of Simon
Kimbangu. When a prophet has been recently active,
and the legend of his actual miracles and expectations
of his future potential are widely diffused and believed

in, then the need for a prophet is awakened. A solution for all problems is now canvassed, and so this idea— the idea of a prophet—becomes a significant social and cultural item. It is not, of course, inconceivable that charismatic demand may occur without the direct experience of a prophet. The idea of a divinely inspired saviour, a cultural hero, or a genius, is certainly widespread, but just how widespread is not easily determined. But even in cultures with a strong tradition of messianic belief, there may well be periods of settled life, when discontents are not so acute, and deprivations not so much in the forefront of human experience, and when the vision of the inspired saviour is dimmed. Man may not always be open to the attraction of a promised superman. Little, local problems may loom larger than the more general evil afflicting a whole community, class, or society. And for little, local problems there may well be tried, legitimated solutions which explain and "contain" them.[53]

Wherever Christianity (or Islam or Judaism) has spread, the idea of fundamental social problems being solved through the instrumentality of a messiah is a theodic possibility that must at once be added to the social repertoire of "coping devices." Whatever other solutions are locally available, whatever expectations are entertained about the part which the ancestors or other agents might play in man's affairs, the idea of a messiah now exists as a projective scheme for the future. In these instances, then, the idea of the divinely

53. On the range of soteriological possibilities, see Bryan R. Wilson, *Magic and the Millennium* (London: Heinemann, and New York, Harper & Row, 1973).

empowered agent exists before such a claimant has appeared locally or recently, and perhaps without such a figure having existed in indigenous cultural tradition. Thus it might occur that even without a specific exemplar, a charismatic demand might exist.

Under certain circumstances that demand might crystallize out into some form of collective action which is appropriately called a "movement." Such movements certainly have origins and originators, but the originators are not themselves "leaders" in quite the sense in which the word is normally used. They may initiate social action without being able to supervise its subsequent course. They may, for example, canvass the idea of a coming messiah, and so stimulate the emergence of a movement which in many ways comes into being in anticipation of a leader. It is the leader who has to be conjured up, and the remedy to existing discontents is conceived as being found not in the activity of the movement so much as in the ordinances that the leader will institute on his arrival. The initiators of the rumours that give rise to such movements themselves may not be the claimants of special power, and they may in some circumstances be virtually unidentifiable once the movement has begun.

The social conditions in which such a demand for charisma is likely to be manifested may be briefly indicated. It might be expected in societies where the possibility for differentiation between individuals in respect of life activities is relatively slight, but where wide disparities have been recognized between indigenous material culture and the material culture of outside intruders into local life. Such societies were found among the Melanesians, and many of them were relatively isolated, were small in scale, undeveloped in internal division of labour, and were confronted—as the last primitive societies to meet the sustained impact of white men—by an immeasurably more advanced material and technical culture. Although cultural heroes are certainly known in the mythology of some Melanesian peoples, the low degree of social differentiation was—despite the significance of acquired status—a distinct limitation in the possibility of any man's claim to exceptional charisma. Supernatural power is much more readily credited to the ancestor spirits or to a supposititious figure, a wish-dream of a man coming from another culture, who will radically alter the life chances of local people.

Thus it is that there are examples of vigorous movements in Melanesian society which are not charismatic in the usual sociological meaning of that word—movements brought into being by a known individual who makes (or has made on his behalf) charismatic claims. The lack of profound differentiation between individuals in Melanesian societies, and the low degree of specialization, perhaps make it inevitable that the typical movement should celebrate, not so much the individual of high standing, as the ancestors as a collectivity. It is clearly not appropriate to employ the concept of charisma in such cases, since there is no social relationship of a following with one actual leader whom they regard as divinely inspired.

But the idea of the charismatic man may gain currency in these cultures, perhaps by the diffusion of Christian ideas, even before a plausible claimant has emerged. Movements may arise in anticipation of his coming, and social events are precipitated in anticipation of a new relationship that is to come into being. From the study of Melanesian data, it is easy to see why Worsley should have been prepared to discount the concept of charisma, since movements develop before convincing charismatic leaders have arisen. Yet it must also be said that, although they lack a significant charismatic figure in some of these movements, the idea of just such a messiah is of vital importance. The well-known Jonfrum movement on the island of Tanna is an interesting case because behind a succession of individuals who gained only weak recognition of their own charisma, the idea of the messiah became powerful and persistent.[54]

Although the first message about Jonfrum, who was to save the Tanna Islanders, was given in 1940 by an identifiable native, Manehivi (a native in his thirties with bleached hair and a coat "with gold buttons"), it is also apparent from the persistence of the movement, and from the fact that there were a succession of claimants to the title that Jonfrum was more an awaited messiah than an actual charismatic leader. The movement is comparable to the anticipatory messianic movements of mediaeval Europe.

Through "black-birding," the recruitment of native labour for plantations elsewhere, the Tannese, who numbered about six thousand, had experienced pro-

54. On this movement see the excellent account in Peter Worsley, *The Trumpet Shall Sound,* 2nd ed. (London: McGibbon and Kee, 1968), pp. 152–160.

tracted contact with Europeans, although there had been very few European residents on the island. For some decades they had been "governed" in effect by the Presbyterian mission and agents (alternately English and French) supplied by the authorities of the Condominium. Christianized natives had been settled on mission controlled land, whilst pagans continued to live in the interior. Discontent about the mission control of land was suddenly exacerbated by the Second World War which disrupted the island's economy.

Jonfrum appears to have been identified by some with a god living in the hills in the southern part of the island, by name Karaperamun, but he was also in many respects a Western type superman, who would eventually make the island entirely flat, cause the whites to leave, render European money useless, and restore to the Tannese their youth. Work and sickness would cease, old customs would be restored, and the mission, the government, and the police would be obliged to leave, together with natives from other islands. It is by no means clear where Manehivi had picked up the various elements in his message, but there was undoubtedly a will to believe it. A run on the stores occurred, and the chiefs kept their people away from the Presbyterian mission services, and kava drinking and dancing—prohibited by the mission—were now freely practised.

Manehivi's arrest, deportation, and imprisonment did not quieten the tales of Jonfrum. Later in 1941, another native, Joe Nalpin had appeared as the representative of the native messiah, and the idea that Jon-

frum was indeed Karaperamun, who spoke through
various agents was disseminated.[55] Nalpin demanded
that a house be built for Jonfrum, now referred to as
"king," whom he would bring from America (this
before the United States entered the war). A little later
the sons of Jonfrum were reported to have arrived by
aeroplane. The entry of the Americans into the war,
and their arrival in the South Seas, appeared like the
fulfilment of Jonfrum prophecy. Here were black men
and white men mixing equally; they brought un-
dreamed of quantities of goods; and they displayed im-
mense generosity. A new claimant to the title of Jonfrum emerged, one Neloiag (or Loiag) who, in typical
cargo cult fashion, undertook the building of an air-
field for the Americans. Another claimant to the title
emerged in 1947, and at his instigation his followers
raided the local store and removed price-tags from the
articles on sale.[56]

The exact relation of each of the claimants to the
title of messiah remains unclear, but it seems reason-
able to suggest that this recrudescent movement de-
pended very largely on the invocation of supernatural
power which none of the actual leaders could himself

55. This idea is brought out particularly by G. L. Barrow,
"The Story of Jonfrum," *Corona* (Journal of H.M. Colonial Service) III, 10, (October, 1951): 379–382. Jean Guiart, "Culture
Contact and the John Frum Movement on Tanna, New Hebri-
des," *Southwestern Journal of Anthropology* 12, 1, (Spring, 1956):
105–16, also regarded Jonfrum as a reincarnation of the god,
Karpenmun (Karaperamun).

56. I have relied considerably on the account of Patrick
O'Reilly, " 'Jonfrum' is New Hebridean 'Cargo Cult,' " *Pacific
Islands Monthly* XXI, 6 (January, 1950): 67–70, and XXI, 7
(February, 1950): 59–65.

claim to possess. Given the small population of the island, the room for manoeuvre, socially and psychologically, was small: power had to be derived from remote times or remote places, from the ancestors, or their ancient deity, or from overseas. The idea of charisma, even if it was exercised as a type of derived charisma, underlies the Jonfrum movement. In part the claims of its actual leaders were, of course, met, because natives discovered the extent to which, once they withdrew their consent to being controlled by the government agent and the mission, they escaped control, and could indeed revert to prohibited practices such as drinking and dancing. Conditions in Tanna may not have been conducive to a fully fledged charismatic movement, and in the return to nativistic practices after the impact of the Jonfrum movement, the traditional gerontocratic pattern was reasserted, without the predominance of any one individual.[57] But in the emergence of the movement the stirrings of charismatic appeal are evident.

A perhaps more dramatic instance of the demand for charisma is to be found in the extraordinary President Johnson cult on the island of New Hanover. Wearied by political promises of social improvement which never seemed to materialize, at least half the 7,000 people on this Melanesian island used the opportunity of the election in which they were to vote for a representative to the newly formed House of Assembly for the Territory of Papua and New Guinea, to declare

57. J. Guiart, "Culture Contact and the John Frum Movement."

their faith in only one man, "Johnson of America." Nor was this gesture merely a protest vote: soon after the election the cultists collected nearly $1,000 to be sent to Johnson to pay his travelling expenses to New Hanover. The natives had learned of Johnson from the operation of an American army survey team for whom some of them had worked. "The Americans paid well, shared their food and goods, and were friendly with the natives. . . ." [58] Their behaviour reawakened memories of the generosity of American troops in the Second World War. The leader of America was Johnson: clearly he was the man who would make things work for the New Hanoverians.

Although the cult had much in common with the many earlier cargo cults of Melanesia, in many of which the return of ancestors with cargo was the focus of cult belief, in this case the ancestors were neither invoked nor regarded as particularly relevant. The cultists' attitude was that, ". . . whether or not ancestral spirits knew how to make cargo, it was clear that Americans knew how, and they could teach the people of New Hanover." [59] Although there were promulgators of the story, and collectors of the money which the cultists withheld from their taxes, they behaved more like the "big men" of old: they were not themselves charismatic leaders. "The cult did not have a prophet: it hardly had leaders. Everybody did much as he pleased. . . ." [60] Yet there was if not a clear instance

58. Dorothy K. Billings, "The Johnson Cult of New Hanover," *Oceania* 40, 1, (September, 1969): 13–19.
59. *Ibid.,* p. 15.
60. *Ibid.,* p. 15.

of charisma at work, none the less a powerful charismatic demand—the man who was wanted was the man
who was thought to have led the Americans to their
way of life. The cultists responded to government re-
monstrances in terms summarized by Billings as fol-
lows:

> The Australians have been here many years and have not
> changed us. We are still like our grandfathers. When the
> Germans came, they developed the land. They planted
> all the coconut plantations. That was their work. Then
> the English-speakers came—first the English, then the
> Australians. They taught us to read and write. That is
> all. They said they were going to help us develop our
> place and get money, but that has not happened. First
> they gave us the co-operative society. They said our store
> would soon have plenty, and old people, and sick people,
> and young people without parents would take things free
> from the store. But they were lying. That never hap-
> pened. . . . Then the Australians gave us the Local Gov-
> ernment Council. They said it would save us. They said
> it would [help us to] get money. But we do not see this
> happening. Now who will save us? We do not want the
> Australians to govern us any more. It is time for the
> Americans to come. They will give us, "savvy".[61]

Clearly the islanders realized, by this time, that no
one man, not even the leader of the Americans would
accomplish transformation of their way of life in the
twinkling of an eye. Their demand for him was a
lingering evidence of that element of personal trust
and faith in the exceptional man (who was known only
by the life-style of "his people"). It was already realized that knowledge and indeed work were necessary

61. *Ibid.*, pp. 16–17.

for social transformation: the charismatic figure was now merely the symbol, the figurehead for strongly desired change. The New Hanoverians, expressing their highly attenuated charismatic demand, were already expressing their desire for a transformed system of social, political, and economic organization. The charismatic element persisted as a token of the magic that men preferred to the work and learning that they also knew was now the inevitable cost of social transformation.

3

Conclusions

It must be evident from the foregoing cases that
charisma may radically affect a social situation—not
because of any inherent power in individual men, but
primarily because such power is looked for in particular individuals. Society operates not infrequently by
faith. Charisma may be analogous to a credit system:
given the faith in the currency, in its redeemability in
commodities or services, currency works, whether the
specie is cowrie shells or printed paper. Even the more
abstract forms of banking credit rely on faith of the
same kind. Charisma works in a similar way—at least
for a little time, and in particular social contexts.
Clearly, the specific prophecies of the charismatic
leader normally fail; the type and range of illnesses that
he can miraculously cure are limited; the essential miracles are heard about rather than seen: the expectations
of his followers are always eventually disappointed.
But this is not to say that nothing is achieved.
Charisma is the occasion for social transformation, and
the transformation is itself the result of faith. Whatever a leader attains by his qualities, he succeeds as a
charismatic leader because of the faith reposed in him.

Such faith is, as we have argued, most easily elicited in societies in which human relationships are manifestations of total personal trust in individuals (not, be it noted, in segmentary role performances)—thus most conspicuously in societies little removed from the primitive. The type of trust in the undifferentiated person which is the norm for societies which lack extensive division of labour and well-articulated role systems is exactly that quality which, in respect of a charismatic leader, we have termed *faith*. Thus it is in simple societies that there obtains that basic condition of human consciousness on which the emergence of a charismatic figure depends. But it is also in the most simple societies—in what is perhaps a hypothetical state of normality with few, if any, extraneous influences to promote change—that it is difficult for any individual to rise far above the generality. The local shaman may acquire a high reputation, but in these very simple societies the range of even his special knowledge is unlikely to so far transcend that of his fellow men that he can attain superordinate importance as an individual. We may suppose that without the impress of external events, the growth of anxieties, and the disruption of normal life, there would be little demand for a man of supposed *extraordinary* supernatural power, and that it would be difficult for such an individual to arise. Once a society has experienced events of this kind, however, the impulse to look for such a man to deal with the new evils appears to grow almost as a normality in itself. This is so because in such societies men do not—indeed cannot—conceive of their problems as susceptible to any solution except through magical and supernatural agencies: and such sources of solutions can be made available only through some man who introduces or (as more easily conceived in such societies) embodies, such power.

Clearly in primitive societies that have experienced sustained disruption in which human anxiety has become an endemic circumstance, heightened periodically by the experience of new evils or the intensification of old ones, a tradition of looking for such a saviour, or listening to prophets, may have arisen. The existence of myths of a coming king, a sleeping warrior, a returning cultural hero, may be regarded—without making too fine a metaphysical quality of it—as a tradition of credibility awaiting arousal. Sometimes there are expectations that, at some future time, faith will be reawakened, and often a prophet—if he succeeds in nothing else—prophesies, and thereby stimulates, future prophets. Such instances, found from Brazil to Indonesia, indicate the significance of charisma in human history, but the basis of charisma is less the quality of the actual leader who comes to be called charismatic, than the will to believe, which, at least in less sophisticated societies (but, at least partially, also in others), awaits the emergence of a suitable object of faith.

Whilst we have no way of knowing whether, in the simplest of societies, and in societies which had not experienced any cultural contact with more advanced peoples, charismatic leaders often or ever, held sway we can, none the less, regard this expression of dependence on some man of extraordinary ability and inspiration as a *relatively* primitive trait, often found among very simple peoples soon after the normal pattern of their social organization and social relationships have once been disturbed. Its continuance in the modern world is itself a testimony to the persistence of simple wish-dreams even among men in complex, technically advanced, and intellectually sophisticated societies. Charisma is an attractive and powerful force. The strength of the will to believe in the exceptional, divinely inspired saviour, the man who can put things right again, has been abundantly evident in both mediaeval and advanced societies.

We have already introduced the concept of charismatic demand, and that concept itself serves as something of a corrective of the use of the appellation "charismatic" to describe what is no more than a forceful, vigorous, or inspiring individual. Once the idea of a great leader arises in society, charismatic demand comes into being. A willingness exists—undoubtedly very differentially distributed among different sections of a population—to believe in the possibility that superordinate competences may be possessed by some divinely designated individual. The demand is essentially simple. It is the easiest and perhaps the most natural recourse for men when in distress—to believe that a father will come and save them. Such faith in immanent power is more primitive than mere faith in a transcendental, invisible god, and certainly more reassuring than confidence that such a god works in inscrutable ways. These last-mentioned propositions are the relatively sophisticated rationalizations and legitimations that prevail in cultures in which men are not only accustomed to disappointment in their dealings with

the gods but in which the demand for consistent commitment has led to the development of a whole religious and cultural tradition to cope with these disap-
pointments. Faith in a transcendental *Ausgleich* is even
more a fabrication of hope where no empirical bases for
hope exist.[1] Against all this the idea of a charismatic
leader is more immediately appealing. He is a man
who is there to be seen, whose works are known, and
who summons confidence in his promise.

The demand for charisma is not necessarily a rejection of alternative devices by means of which order
may be brought back into human affairs. No alternative procedure may be canvassed, or even known. In
simple societies, in which men express their compre-
hension of phenomena and events in the personal
idiom, in which abstract concepts are not employed
and in which there is a consequent inability to distinguish facts from values, the establishment (or re-estab-
lishment) of order appears to depend solely on the intervention of some powerful individual.[2] Causal
analysis of a social situation; collective organization;
conscious community decision-making; the logistics of
devising social action; the very idea that by "taking
thought" men can indeed amend their social circumstances—are all unknown possibilities. It is not merely
that material techniques are undeveloped, but that
social organization is necessarily unconscious and

1. The transcendental *Ausgleich* is discussed by Talcott Parsons, *The Social System* (London: Tavistock 1952), pp. 372–374.

2. The implications of this point for religion are discussed in
Bryan R. Wilson, *Secularization* (Oxford, Blackwell, and New
York, Harper and Row), forthcoming.

"given." [3] Since community life, custom, and economic techniques are themselves heavily endowed with supernatural sanction, so their conscious amendment becomes in itself unthinkable—but, with the emergence of a charismatic figure, a wide range of practices and procedures, even though they are sacrally reinforced, may be suddenly abandoned and superseded. It is in this sense, of course, that the charismatic man displays his power, in daring to set himself over against the accumulated weight of divinely charged custom. It is the radical relocation of faith, the belief in him, which establishes charisma as the catalyst which will transform the complex web of social intercourse and organization. For whatever the specific "platform" of a prophet, be it innovation or restoration, charisma produces social change. It "works."

It "works" by providing the basis—sometimes, given the prevailing level of social knowledge, the only basis—for change. But there is another sense, clearly, in which the causal element in charisma is radically mistaken. The charismatic figure is often the man in terms of whom a society can take stock of itself and of its position, within the framework of the simple causal assumptions which they have not, as yet, transcended. He sets forth what is wrong. And more important, he says what must be done. What is attributed to the divine endowment of the leader, is achieved by the faith of his followers—albeit sometimes specifically at

3. An instance of this is given very forcefully by David Riesman, in the Introduction to Daniel Lerner, *The Passing of Traditional Society: Modernizing the Middle East* (Glencoe, Ill.: Free Press, 1958), p. 3.

his prompting. It is in this sense that charisma is a manifestation of the simplest mode of the "social construction of reality"—that mode which attributes action to the man's volition, and most especially to the divine man's volition. In this sense, charisma comes straight from the context of savagery, from the simplest forms of society. Even though by no means all the charismatic leaders discussed in the foregoing pages were themselves savages, and even though the societies in which they operated were not entirely savage, in that, in some cases, a measure of literacy and advanced techniques had been introduced to at least some of their followers, none the less it is not inappropriate to regard charismatic leaders as men for whom is claimed a nobility that arises from an entirely savage framework of thought.

The Cultural Conditions for Charismatic Leadership

The persistence of charismatic demand has already become apparent from cases reviewed above. These cases stand for many others, in some of which the very terms of the charismatic claim and the style of the charismatic figure have shown little change over long periods. Whereas Kimbangu's successors varied their specific claims, and led their followers in various directions, with a growing undercurrent of African nationalism beneath the waves of magico-religious practice, elsewhere—for example, in the Manseren movement in Biak, north-west New Guinea—prophets arose at frequent intervals over the course of several decades with, apparently, only a very gradual shift of emphasis from magical to political concerns, and even then with a strong persistence of fundamentally magical ideas.[4] In certain conditions of society, charismatic demand has its equivalent in recurrent charisma. We need not discuss here the well-known issues of the instability of charisma; the difficulty for prophets in fulfilling their promises, and the problems of the institutionalization of charisma. All these difficulties are conducive to the occurrence of recurrent charismatic claims. In some cases, and the Belgian Congo exemplified this in the aftermath of Kimbangu, it is not inappropriate to refer to the demand for charismatic leadership as endemic.

Although general social malaise is undoubtedly the primary condition for the persistence of charismatic manifestations, and the best sustenance for charismatic demand, the operation of a "successful" prophet is also a powerful stimulant. Kimbangu was "successful." There are no properly attested miracles, although some of his converts, interviewed decades later, claimed healings. But his success was not so much in his actual operation as in the reputation he acquired. He was arrested before doubt had set in among his followers, and the best charismatic claims were made *for* him rather than *by* him. His arrest, trial, and death sentence set the seal of martyrdom on his career, whilst the commutation of the death sentence to life imprisonment,

4. On the Manseren movement, see F. C. Kamma *De Messiaanse Koreribewegingen in het Biake-Noemfoorse Cultuurgebied* (The Hague: Voorhoeve, 1954); J. M. van der Kroef, "Patterns of Cultural Change in Three Primitive Societies," *Social Research* 24, 4 (Winter, 1957): 427–456; Peter Worsley, *The Trumpet Shall Sound* (London: McGibbon & Kee, 1957), pp. 126–130.

indicated the quality of the power of "the man they dared not kill." Once such a successful charismatic leader has existed, the myth is always there to be reactivated, at least until the society "grows out" of its belief in charisma and seeks real solutions to social situations. (For although the charismatic figure may dramatically affect society, and set processes of rapid social change into motion—as occurred with both Harris and Kimbangu in the elimination, at least temporarily, of belief in fetiches—he does not, of course, analyse real social problems and provide planned solutions.)

The speed with which different societies "grow out" of their belief in charisma is of course dependent on a large number of factors. There is a sense, certainly, in which men never grow out of the belief, although in advanced society the role and operation of charisma do become very much modified. But even among much more primitive societies, differences are to be observed in the way in which initial faith in charismatic figures may be amended. Anything approaching a complete analysis of such differences would require detailed information about a wide range of social and cultural conditions, but some possible sources of the differences can be indicated.

The North American Indians appear to have remained for long periods impressed by the possibilities of messianic intervention in their affairs, and at times such ideas gained dramatic dominance. The slowness of the process of cultural contact, the scale of the continent over which it occurred, and the increased association between tribes may account for the persistence of strong dispositions of charismatic demand among them. Melanesians, however, appear to have at least moderated their assumptions about charisma in very much shorter time, and even in the Manseren movement in Biak, which was persistently recrudescent, six or seven decades appears to have seen its force wax and finally wane. The President Johnson cult on New Hanover was a touching instance of charismatic demand without supply, but even in its full expression it was already a highly pragmatic modification of traditional charisma. The cultists wanted technical knowledge, and although naïve in their assumptions about how to attain it, given what they knew about Americans and what they were taught to expect from the political process, they made not unreasonable inferences. In the event, it did not take much to introduce the cultists to a practical work programme which—if more slowly— at least began to bring them toward the benefits that they demanded from their putative charismatic leader.

The materialistic concerns of Melanesian cultures, and the relatively less-developed concepts of leadership in these societies may have further muted the extent of their reliance on charisma in this and other cases, and may also have facilitated the shift from supramundane to practical activities among the charismatic cultists in several Melanesian cases (the Irakau movement; the Paliau movement on Manus; and the Tommy Kabu movement in the Purari Delta, are examples).[5]

5. For a detailed account of the Paliau Movement, see Theodore Schwarz, "The Paliau Movement in the Admiralty Islands," *Anthropological Papers of the American Museum of Natural History,*

In Africa, charisma has clearly an older and more respectable history. The very size of tribes in some parts of the continent; the long process of effective conquest and migration (for the like of which we have not the same sort of substantial evidence in Melanesia); and the traditions of warrior-kings are all items from which charismatic demand might be derived. The long-sustained influence of Islam, with its own messianic tradition of Mahdism, cannot be ignored. Nor indeed, can the effect of long exposure, at least along the coastline, to Christianity, with its own model of a god-man saviour, and with missionaries, many of whom have been exponents of second advent teachings. Christianity of any stripe might indeed stimulate charismatic demand. The anthropomorphic style in which Christian faith is often presented, with considerable ambiguity concerning the operation of the Spirit in this life, communication with the Father or the Son, the intercession of Saints, and the possibility of the Son's return to earth, might all reinforce charismatic expectations, just as they did in mediaeval Europe.[6] The case of Kimbangu himself is not without significance for such

---

49, Pt. 2, 1962; On Tommy Kabu, see R. F. Maher, *New Men of Papua* (Madison: University of Wisconsin Press, 1961). For a brief account of the two movements and an analysis of their social significance, see Bryan R. Wilson, *Magic and the Millennium* (London: Heinemann, and New York: Harper and Row, 1973).

6. See Norman Cohn, *Pursuit of the Millennium* (London: Secker and Warburg, 1957). The mediaeval movements with which Cohn deals are primarily messianic in character, centering around a charismatic figure: the millennium is one item in a messianic vocabulary in many of these cases.

an argument, since the prophet so persistently imi-
tated Jesus.

The Persistence of Charisma

The likelihood of a socially significant manifestation
of charisma undoubtedly diminishes with technical advance. The charismatic myth itself loses cogency in
societies in which sophisticated historical knowledge is
well diffused and in which there is a body of sociological and psychological understanding available to explain particular social situations, and technical means
of providing solutions for social problems. Yet the
charismatic idea does not die entirely. Despite the
growth of modern scepticism, promoted and disseminated by the mass media, the appeal of the charismatic
persists—as the media's *penchant* for the word itself tes-
tifies. Its source of strength is precisely also the cause
of its weakness: it stands over against modern sophis-
tication as something crude and primitive, but simultaneously as something fundamental and radical. Over
against contemporary dependence on complex techniques and intellectualism it sets the appeal of simplic-
ity, ultimacy, and primary virtues.

The charismatic leader is strongest in appealing to
primitive needs, and certainly those charismatics who
have arisen in more advanced societies whose claims to
charisma have been least inhibited have usually ex-
tolled primary virtues, and have offered their own
primitivism as a token of the better world that has
been lost, and which, by trust in them, might be restored. The virtues which charismatic leaders canvass,

when charisma attains a level of exemplary and prescriptive ethical concern, are the virtues of interpersonal face-to-face relationships. Men are exhorted to love one another, to forgive one another (at least within the in-group, and perhaps beyond it) and to recognize the brotherhood of the faithful. These virtues are, of course, indispensable for the orderly conduct of human relations, but they are by no means an adequate guide to conduct in highly impersonal bureaucratic and technological social contexts. This in itself is an indication of both the attractiveness and the inadequacy of charismatic appeal to primal virtues. The rhetoric of charisma employs an earthy vocabulary of body imagery and basic biological elements. In these terms the in-group is reassured of itself and its boundaries, and its being as a "natural" entity. It is no accident that Hitler's ideological repertoire drew so heavily on race, blood, ruralism, primary native virtue, pre-Christian religious imagery, folk values, and semi-mystical atavism. Nor is it mere political expediency that causes African leaders—themselves sometimes disposed to believe in charisma, and often deriving their charismatic style from the office they assume—to emphasize *negritude.* The idea of racial qualities has an appeal at a more emotive level than the advocacy of particular instrumental, rational, or technical procedures and planning, which reduce the basis for preferring one leader to another to such residual items as mere physical attraction, qualities of temperament, or incidentals of style.

In contrast, progressive, rationalistic, and technically oriented ideologies, among which orthodox

Marxism is the prototype, reject charisma as atavistic, irrational mystification which needlessly obscures, with infantile and romantic fancies, the "real" factors at work in social development, and the "real" principles of social organization. Although not all Marxist leaders have escaped the imputation of charismatic influence, and the analogies between the Russian treatment of Lenin and Catholic hagiography have frequently been noticed, it is clear that a Marxist theory of history necessarily militates against the concept. There is, of course, a certain unclarity in the position. Because Marxists look for "real" causes in the explanation of historical processes, and because they themselves dismiss charisma as a figment of false consciousness, they may, and sometimes do, blind themselves to the fact that the collective belief of men in the divine inspiration of a particular individual has influenced social affairs in any degree. Thus they are disposed to deny themselves the benefit of what is a very common observation about men and society. One may oneself reject a "great man theory" of history whilst recognizing that mankind at large has believed in it, and that that belief is a historical fact which has itself influenced the course of history. The primitive will to believe in great men, and in the supernatural has had—and may in some measure still have—considerable effect on social development. That this is not the main factor promoting social change is evident, but even in modern times it is still a factor—and the more primitive the level of social consciousness in a given culture, the more appeal is the idea of charismatic leadership likely to have.

The likelihood of charismatic leaders (who are not of course to be confused with leaders whom the mass media lightly label "charismatic") emerging at the political level in the modern West has undoubtedly diminished. In part, this is so because of the diffusion of Marxist thinking throughout the Western world, and its infiltration into public attitudes and sentiments. More significantly, however, it is so because of the acclimatization of men in modern societies to a wide variety of daily more pervasive technical procedures— which are themselves the encapsulation of sophisticated and cumulative rationality. It would perhaps be rash, following Hitler—the last man to succeed by unrestrained appeal to the primitive, romantic, and atavistic passions of men—to declare with too little qualification that there will not be another charismatic leader who will capture the power of the state in Western countries. Yet, conditions similar to those in which Hitler emerged are unlikely to recur, and the dependence of men on rationalized systems in both technology and bureaucracy must—for most men and in the major institutional spheres of society—put the charismatic at a discount, even in times of extreme distress. Those unique circumstances included the persistence of rural and romantic ideals in a technically advanced, but temporarily collapsed society, and the shock of national defeat and cultural degradation for a people who had long been deeply committed to an only recently realized nationalist ideal.

The growth of technology and of our dependence upon it, has put personal trust at a discount: we rely on role performances and duly certificated competences, rather than on the innate—much less on the divinely endowed—qualities of individuals. We rely very largely on men as technical agents rather than as moral agents. Moral standards, as judged by levels of disinterested goodwill, detached commitment, and universalistic objectivity have undoubtedly risen over the long course of human history. The development of these attributes among the generality of men in all the public spheres of their activity has been indispensable to the growing dependence of society on role performances. A general morality of an impersonal kind is taken for granted as the basis on which the exercise of specialist competences implicitly relies. The growth of this type of disinterested goodwill (which, following a variety of changes in contemporary practices in the socialization of individuals, may itself be jeopardized—although this is not our concern here) has led to a reduction in our reliance on specifically personal attributes. We no longer need to trust the total person as was the case before society acquired elaborate division of labour and highly specific roles. Personal qualities are of less consequence, personal differences for actual tasks and performances lose, in many departments, their once primary significance. These changes naturally affect the prospect of a charismatic claimant. We do not now expect the exceptional man to solve our problems: we turn rather to our cumulative resources, stored up in a social inheritance of complex, interdependent competences and equipment.

The changing attitudes, in the course of the last century, to the moral misdemeanours of national leaders is another evidence in the same direction. The politician employs a moral rhetoric to inspire confidence. The tone of that morality has necessarily passed from terms of group-righteousness to more objective and universalistic claims. Inevitably, given the foibles of even great leaders, and the increasing capacity of the mass media to probe them, the stature of politicians, in the moral terms of our own times, is diminished. Lacking distinctive class legitimations to be above normal morals and normal mortals (such as a Palmerston might have enjoyed), but needing to use an impersonal, detached moral language, the consequence for politicians is their loss of credibility. Freudian psychology, image projection, democratic and egalitarian ideals join the media of communication to discourage the feeling—common in primitive and mediaeval societies—that supreme power must be associated with great personal virtue. Then, of course, power and virtue reposed in monarchs or priest-kings rather than in politicians: it was they whose sanctity cured illnesses, whose wisdom transcended that of ordinary men, whose mistakes were necessarily due to bad or evil advisers.[7] Modern politicians need less claim to virtue, or even to moral probity: although politics is scarcely an exact or technical science, the political man has become more dependent on a mixture of techniques than on his quality as a person. The bases of political survival among the leaders of democratic

7. On priesthood and kingship see Marc Bloch, *The Royal Touch: Sacred Monarchy and Scrofula in England and France* (London: Routledge, 1973), and Werner Stark, *Sociology of Religion,* vol. III, *The Universal Church* (London: Routledge, 1967), pp. 11–248.

parties might be reduced—were the cases impartially examined—to a mixture of image projection; cynical self-seeking; ruthless ambition; cleverness; some technical competences in economic or diplomatic matters; a measure of ideological commitment (in which however the virtue of consistency is often sacrificed for exigent reasons); and a patchy residue of personality characteristics. That politicians must use moral rhetoric is itself almost anachronistic—the failure of the technicians to produce an alternative language of persuasion with which to manipulate the masses in democratic societies. Of course, the language changes somewhat: the rotund morally suffused sentiments of a Gladstone or a Bryan have a different ring from the more anaemic moral tones in which a Nixon, a Brandt, or a Heath address their publics. Yet a moral rhetoric is the only language of common communication for publics that demand a measure of social control and that must be cajoled into additional work efforts, the payment of more taxes, and support for political office-holders. But they, despite the rhetoric, no more believe in the innate, untutored virtue of their national people than their people believe it of them. The basis of confidence that comprises the charismatic relationship is no longer there, and it appears unlikely to be recovered.

In the modern world the idea of the charismatic persists, of course, but it has largely passed beyond the margins of political activity. Journalists appropriate the word as an impressive alternative for *glamour*. The concept is diluted. Equally, the demand for charisma has diminished, except as a titillation. Like magic, mystery, and the occult, it is not accepted seriously on its own terms, but as a trivial and marginal fascination. The marginalities may be of different kinds, of course: the marginal leisure hours of the otherwise seriously occupied, or in the marginal groups (the leisured, under-employed middle-aged women, or the young as yet unanchored in secure role obligations). Even in the abundant charismatic cults there is a well-recognized divorce between real social power and the faith in the supernatural—the charismatic leader exercises his power only within the circumscribed arena of his own voluntary movement. The largest and fastest cult movements in the Western world, do not grow around a particular charismatic claimant, but there are many small movements led by charismatic figures. Whereas in mediaeval societies and in primitive societies, whole communities were sometimes drawn into messianic enthusiasms, which briefly encompassed people's entire life activities, in modern societies the belief in charisma is more sectional, confined to particular spheres of activity, and generally less ecstatic in its effect. Votaries are more self-consciously and more individually self-selected. Their commitment—and paradoxically this may in itself evidence the attenuation of charismatic appeal—is likely to be sustained over a longer time. The adherents of contemporary claimants to divine inspiration or to deity are predominantly the young or the members of a particular ethnic constituency (as, for instance, Father Divine's Peace Mission or the Black Muslims).

The power of cult figures is clearly circumscribed. Their "miracles" rarely appear to transcend the immediate circumstances of their own needs and those of their followers. Modern Western man, more used to pragmatic and empirical procedures, is necessarily a less credulous man. If marginal groups still believe in miracles then, compared to men in earlier and less-developed societies, they believe only in small miracles. These are the faint evidences of lingering persistence of charismatic demand, and even this demand is compromised by modern conditions.

Modern charismatic movements, we have noted, tend to persist longer than did the brief enthusiasms of the Delaware Prophet and Tenskwatawa; they display more stability than the persistently recrudescent cargo cults of Biak and Tanna. The cost of their durability is a process of institutionalization. The antithesis of charisma, as Weber expounded the concept, is found in routine, stability, and in regular, integrated institutional procedures. But in some of the new cult movements which acclaim a single charismatic figure there is undoubtedly a considerable measure of routinization. Modern society has devices that—at least to all appearances—can reconcile the appeal of the charismatic with the steady operation of a bureaucratic organization. The modern charismatic leader displays the expected spontaneity, whimsicality, and unpredictability: but behind him often stands not so much a circle of disciples as a trained cadre of officials, whose roles are well defined within a clearly articulated and relatively bureaucratic structure. Their concern is publicity and the projection of the charismatic image, but also the protection of the movement from undue charismatic eccentricity. Charismatic persistence is, paradoxically, facilitated by procedures which are the antithesis of the cause to which they are harnessed. Nor is this relation merely a stage in the process which Weber discussed, the institutionalization of charisma: it may be a persisting accommodation of circumscribed charisma and concealed bureaucratic power. Even semi-charismatic figures, borrowing the charisma of their message rather than proclaiming themselves as messiahs or even as prophets, have not infrequently been "tricked" by the bureaucratic underpining of the movements that they brought into being.[8] It is only in less-developed societies that charisma can arise and flourish untrammelled by institutional compromises. Only there are the primary virtues of the supposedly socially undetermined (that is the supposedly un-socialized) man, recognizable and attractive. Such is the self-awareness of modern man and his belief in conscious social planning, that for that primitive faith, charisma, to exist in modern society, it must be supported and compromised by the very agencies against which its basic thrust should be directed.

Charisma and Cult Movements

Not all recent and contemporary cult leaders in Western societies have been drawn from marginal ethnic groups or from alien societies (in the later class Majarij Ji; his Divine Grace Swami Bhakti Vedanta of

8. See, for example, the case of George Jeffreys, founder of the British Pentecostal sect, the Elim Church, in Bryan R. Wilson, *Sects and Society* (London: Heinemann, and Berkeley and Los Angeles: University of California Press, 1961), pp. 37–56.

the Hare Krishna cult; Sun Myung Moon, of the Unified Family are the most conspicuous examples), but
their prominence and relative success when compared
with such figures as Louwrens van Voorthuizen (Lou)
in Holland, Georges Roux in France, and Oskar Ernst
Bernhardt in Germany and Austria, all of whom
claimed to be the messiah—is striking. In advanced
Western society, it appears that claims to real
charisma, if they are to succeed, must be supported by
exotic provenance. Perhaps the sources of indigenous
romantic feeling have now themselves grown too weak
to sustain a charismatic claim from the indigenous
Western tradition: the cultural context is an incongru-
ous breeding ground for miracle-men. Not only is God
not born in Surbiton or Yonkers, but the whole aura of
mystery, supernatural power, superordinate experience, and hitherto unknown wisdom, cannot be recon-
ciled with the experience of a civilization that depends
on computers, electronics, data retrieval systems,
time-and-motion studies, and cost-benefit analysis. If
God is alive *he must* come from a society that is still
traditional, unplanned, unprogrammed, and in which
arcane mystery, and occult philosophy may still
flourish. The real savage, if such still exists, is too
remote, his emotional tone and thought processes too
obscure: but antique civilizations remain, resistant to
modernity and a persisting source for the cultural borrowing of charismatic inspiration.

That the soil of Western society is uncongenial for
the growth of indigenous charisma is evidenced, too,
by the changing character of Western sectarianism—
that area of social phenomena in which charisma might

most readily be expected to be apparent. There are no sizeable sects of Western origin which compare with the recently imported Eastern charismatic movements. Old-style Western sects are not charismatic. But even they—in looking back to a style of personal life in which high moral virtues flourished and to a time in which the moral capital of our "ideal values" was accumulated—grow less and less congenial to their modern social context. But there are also sects of a newer style. Instead of the emphasis on community and personal moral worth, they celebrate the most secular values of Western society; rest their appeal very largely on the aid they provide to people who are fighting their way through the system; and claim to support modern man psychologically, in the pursuit of his materialistic aims. They validate the pragmatic, instrumental values of contemporary society. Although they may utilize old devices of legitimation, and may, in their battery of publicity techniques, even claim charismatic virtue for their leadership, none the less the main thrust of movements such as Psychiana, Christian Science, Unity, and Scientology has been the reinforcement of the secular goals of their votaries and the means for their achievement. These newer-style sects are scarcely less secular than the societies in which they emerge. This shift in religious style indicates the growing implausibility of indigenous charismatic claims.

Yet it is clear that however dependent are modern societies on bureaucracy, technology, and conscious planning, the appeal of the charismatic does not entirely die. Not only are the fringe cults from the

Orient with their youthful following an evidence of
this, but in a very dilute form a residue of charismatic
demand—perhaps *hankering* is a more suitable word
—persists. Whilst the orthodox, de-charismatized
churches steadily lose influence and support and the
new cults develop, in the religious penumbra there
have persisted, during the last century, echoes of
charisma. And outside the sphere of religion itself,
there has also been an appropriation of something akin
to charismatic phenomena. These echoes and stirrings
are of three recognizable varieties which may justify
the qualification of the gross concept *charisma* into the
sub-species of derived charisma and diffused charisma,
and occasion the recognition of an associated phenomenon—extra-religious inspiration.

Derived Charisma

Derived charisma is merely the attenuated claim of
the latter-day prophet. An institutionalized, originally
charismatic faith persists largely by periodic calls to
remember the original message (or something that
passes for the original message). In such revivalistic
terms, new miracles may be worked, usually in the
name of the original charismatic claimant (occasionally
in the name of the ancestors). Even though the charismatic leader is only remembered, his name is invoked
and reinvoked by men who may borrow the patina of
charisma. The modern prophet in the Christian tradition, typically the revivalist, enjoys an element of
quasi-charisma, but he is quick to point to the name in
which he claims to speak, and to emphasize that the

message is not of his own making. The prophet may even reinterpret his own role to attune to the expectations of modern men: to prophesy, the revivalists may say, is not to foretell but to forth-tell. Thus the role of the prophet is reduced to that of the preacher—albeit a preacher who regards himself as uniquely called and perhaps specially equipped by God for the role he has appropriated.

Revivalists frequently claim healings, particularly during the revival campaigns which they conduct (much less so in the ordinary church life of their community): it is the revivalist, apparently, whose presence is conducive to healing. That this should be so need not surprise us, given the intensification of emotions which is often induced in revivals. But such healings are themselves an evidence of superordinate power—a faint manifestation of the charismatic, of the special relation of faith between leader and followers, which in this instance may be of such brief duration that it does not outlive the occasion of the revival meeting itself. For the revival is presented as a highly uninstitutionalized event, an occasion for the operation of the Holy Spirit among men. Although there is, and must be, elaborate organization for such a campaign, as far as possible such organization remains concealed. The organizers appear to be well aware that the very fact of organization tarnishes the revivalist image and interferes with even that vestigial element of the charismatic which the occasion seeks to summon. The claims of the revivalist not only do not depend on organization, but are in large measure antithetical to them. Newspaper stories about the scale, style, and monetary costs of the organization for revivals, far from being regarded as desirable publicity by revivalists, are put forward as a derogation of revivalistic claims.[9]

The revival must not proceed as routine: its necessary bureaucratic supports must be hidden. This becomes most evident in the way in which financial support is mustered for the revivalist. Who shall set a monetary price on the value of one soul saved, or one body healed? The services of the revivalist clearly cannot be assessed on any scale of agreed reimbursement. That would be to make him a paid agent, a salaried official, when his whole image depends on the claim to harness supernatural power. His reward must be equally charismatic, and although it is usually solicited in a carefully planned manner, a charismatic style is created. Toward the end of such a campaign, the evening's proceedings will be a little late in beginning. The revivalist will not be in evidence, but a local minister will call for a hymn. Then he will comment on the blessings of the campaign and praise the revivalist: he will ask the audience how many have been saved, or healed, or blessed, doing his best to awaken enthusiastic recognition. He will then point out that the revivalist has come a long way, and left his own normal work in the care of another, to donate his time and exercise his spiritual gifts. Everyone who has benefitted will want to make a powerful gesture of recognition

9. The number of serious studies of revivalism are few, but see W. G. McLoughlin Jr., *Modern Revivalism* (New York: Ronald Press, 1959). On the other hand, the *exposé* of revivalism has been frequently attempted, especially in journalistic vein. A recent example of this genre, is G. W. Target, *Evangelism, Inc.* (London: Allen Lane, 1968).

to the revivalist. Supported by biblical quotations, "Freely ye have received, freely give," he will announce a special collection. " 'How much shall I give?' you will ask. 'I cannot tell you brother. You know how you have been blessed. You know what you *want* to give. You know what you can *afford* to give. But brother, you can get some advice. Lay the burden on Jesus. Let the Lord direct you. Ask him what you shall give.' " Thus the reward for the revivalist is as charismatic in style as his own activity. Necessary pecuniary arrangements and routine organizational requirements are met, but without impinging on the derived charismatic connotations of the operation.

Diffused Charisma and Democracy

Derived charisma characterized the nineteenth-century revivalist tradition of Western Protestantism. During the century, revivalism underwent a considerable measure of systematization and, despite periodic regressions, a loss of some spontaneity and fervour. Social conditions and the changing life-style and consciousness of urban man, made the re-evocation of primitive Christian charisma increasingly difficult. Among a small minority of young people Jesus is still a name to conjure with, of course, and there are still the trappings and accoutrements of revivalism, with some evidences of derived charisma by some contemporary authoritarian leaders.

The central thrust of social and political development, however, has, in all Western countries, been toward increased democratic participation (in however token a form) and egalitarianism (in strict monetary terms, if not in cultural and social terms). The ideological justification for these developments is that men are not very unequal in natural endowment, and that environmental and educational provision can be equalized, even perhaps to a point where nurture will "correct" nature in regard to such inequalities as might naturally exist. Superordinate qualities are not reckoned with in such a framework of social planning: charisma is regarded as a spent force. The system disregards it, and individuals are socialized to discount it. Yet, as we have observed, even complete egalitarianism appears unlikely to eliminate our discontents, and may not even diminish their sum total. Boredom with routinized operations is a powerful factor in modern society, and the persistence of a gap, perhaps even of a widening gap, between stimulated aspirations (now diffused among much wider strata of the population) and the possibility of their attainment, makes the final eclipse of the demand for novelty, spontaneity, and the unplanned, unprogrammed happening seem highly unlikely. Yet, with so many promises, boredom has come to be regarded as intolerable. In the past, when life was harder, boredom may have been less common, but in any case, the threshold of expectations was lower. The world still had its mysteries, justifying—however abominably to our modern view—inequalities, random fortune, and diversity. Boredom in recent years has doubtlessly played its part not only in the heightening of sexual titillation in entertainment, but also in the spread of the use of drugs; the enthusiasm among the young for the "demo"; the promotion of the "love-in" and the happening; and in the search at the periphery of our society for new sources of meaning, for new contact with something primary and savage—epitomized so fully in the recourse to sexual exploration among complete strangers in the sensitivity training groups. Contemporary dabbling in the occult, in witchcraft, in tarot cards, even, in the case of a Charles Manson and some others like him, in murder, cannot be ignored in seeking to assess the success of the modern man's endeavours to remake his world.

All these manifestations of enterprise occur in the interstitial areas of the social system, in those (perhaps expanding) contexts and periods in which men are unregulated, and unfettered either by agencies of social control, or the inhibitions and self-discipline created by the rigorous processes of socialization which were the lot of at least the more educated sections of society in the past. It is not surprising that among these phenomena echoes of charisma may also be heard. Charisma, too, is part of the tradition of a more romantic world, even if it has no greater possibility of withstanding severe scrutiny than have the feeble magics of the highly organized entertainment industry or the publishing house. But charisma has itself not been unaffected by the democratic egalitarianism of the times, and its chief manifestation in the modern world is as the diffusion of supernatural power, available to all. The modern neo-Pentecostal movement itself uses (no doubt in the theological sense) the term "charismatic renewal." Drawing one stratagem from the plethora of Christian possibilities, in effect it necessarily makes less of the unique charisma of Jesus, and more of the diffused charisma bequeathed to his followers. The Holy Spirit must be the central reference point for this development (however much, and perhaps as a conpensatory claim to theological orthodoxy, classical, sectarian Pentecostalism came to emphasize and re-emphasize its own Jesucentricity). Whatever the formal doctrinal statement of "charismatic renewal," however, and whatever the language in which "power" is claimed, the logic of Pentecostalism, of acquiring power to speak in unknown tongues, to prophesy, to perform miracles, must be in the diffusion of charisma from the Holy Spirit.

In both the older sectarian Pentecostal movement, as it has now spread to embrace millions throughout the world, and in the growing charismatic renewal movement, which is most developed in the United States and other English-speaking countries, men and women are claiming to be touched by the Holy Spirit, to encounter divine power, which is theirs for use in worship, and sometimes in other contexts.[10] The claim is that there is an effusion and a diffusion of superordinate power, available to all to recharge their spirituality and to transform their daily lives, and that this power may be had without transgressing the boundaries of orthodox Christian faith and practice.

10. There is now an extensive literature, if not on the sociology, at least on the history and theology, of Pentecostalism. See for reliable historical accounts, Nils Bloch-Hoell, *The Pentecostal Movement* (London: Allen & Unwin, 1964); Walter G. Hollenweger, *The Pentecostals* (London: SCM Press, 1972). For a sociological study, see Luther P. Gerlach and Virginia M. Hine, *People, Power, Change* (Indianapolis: Bobbs Merrill, 1970).

What is gone, of course, is the concept of charismatic *leadership,* and with it the idea that supernatural power would alter society and the world. Charisma in the Pentecostal movement is personal and congregational, experienced mainly as men draw out of the world and into an enclave of sanctity. The claim made for this diffused charismatic experience is that it sanctifies individual lives. But even when widely diffused this measure of sanctity appears not to alter the objective conditions, but only the subjective orientations of its recipients. Thus even the basic element in charismatic leadership—of a social relationship between the charismatic claimant and the mass of men is considerably modified. The speaker in tongues may gain the credence of the rest of the congregation. The message, when interpreted (by divine power) may be received. But the manifestation of faith in charisma is so narrowly circumscribed, and so inconsequential for objective conditions beyond the assembly in which it occurs that, whatever may be the justification theologically for the use of the term, only the most attenuated residue of what sociologists mean by *charisma* is apparent in this situation.

In an age that relies increasingly on technical knowledge there is a profound hiatus between charisma and leadership. Charisma, in the sense of divine inspiration, no longer justifies the claim to leadership. Conversely, leaders, even of religious organizations, rarely claim charisma as the basis for their position, their opinions, or their policies. In a society in which religious institutions, practice, and ways of thinking have all diminished, the idea of divine inspiration is pushed to the periphery of experience. It is privatized, or it occurs only in those cults that are regarded by the majority as entirely marginal or even as frivolous and bizarre.

Yet there are still figures, even in the context of technical and secular societies, who can establish a type of relationship with followers which is strongly reminiscent of the charismatic. Short on both counts—the explicit affirmation of divine inspiration, and the ability to exercise effective leadership in more than inconsequential ways, this phenomenon scarcely qualifies for inclusion in a discussion of charisma. It may be justified only if we regard it as a manifestation of charismatic demand and the approximation of a reply, qualified by the conditions of the modern world. The phenomenon is, of course, the mass appeal of the popular entertainer, particularly of the young entertainer with a mass audience of adolescents.

The language used of these entertainers echoes— perhaps only in consequence of the debasement of the linguistic coinage by publicity agents—the language of charisma. They are *idols,* their performances are *magic,* their qualities *fantastic* and *fabulous* (now that old charismatic epithets—*angelic, heavenly, divine, enchanting, bewitching* have been worn out). The manifestations of individual ecstasy and group frenzy at their performances perhaps outdo those at the reception of messianic claimants of the past. But such figures enjoy neither political significance nor enduring social regard. They make no specific claims for themselves: they are simply the recipients of extraordinary social acclaim, and the stimulators of extraordinary psychological responses. The term *possession* has been used for the ecstasy manifested by pop fans, and the degree of devotion is not apparently different from that which messianic claimants have aroused. But such is the impoverishment of the imagination in the technical society that even this phenomenon must be carefully manipulated, the responses stimulated by a battery of diverse techniques of publicity, and suggestion. The involvement is segmentary, and even for the participants counts only as "time out," when normal restraints may be abandoned, not as a way of acquiring a new consciousness, or of transcending the mundane requirements and expectations of everyday life, but only as a temporary and almost calculated escape from routine.

The survival of charisma in contemporary society is questionable. The incidence of anything approaching it, occurs at best peripherally and interstitially, almost only as a leisure-time recreational activity, rather than as a dynamic force for innovation and transformation. Charisma is now merely for fun: its public is of fans rather than of followers. If we rule out, as I have done, the persistence of men of goodwill and large spirit, for whose indubitably desirable talents *charisma* is far too powerful a word, then we are left with these marginal cases of derived charisma, diffused charisma, and leaderless charisma. All of them are weak manifestations of what I think is none the less a persisting charismatic demand. It is a demand, however, that cannot be formulated in the terms of authentic charisma: the divine inspiration of the prophet, would scarcely be acceptable in the modern world, least of all if *per impossible* it were authentic!

Charisma has been a force in the social development of many societies, but of most uneven incidence, and often of disastrous consequence. Yet the phenomenon expresses a certain idealism, a will to discover qualities of mind, character, and purpose that are both untutored and undetermined, either by heredity or by environment. The social circumstances in which charisma might be manifested appear to me to have begun in savage societies, to have continued and perhaps become most vigorous in antiquity and in the mediaeval world, and to have rapidly waned following the development of advanced industrial society. A whole range of primary virtues have passed away, if not in fact at least in their social significance. They may, of course, have never really existed in any powerful form, except perhaps as they were ephemerally evoked in the charismatic relationship—in the moments of Durkheim's *social effervescence*. But that something approaching them could be envisaged or half attained in everyday life may have been not unconnected with the mistaken gesture of faith that charisma implies. There may never have been any noble savages, but the idea that there were—as long as we could believe in it—may have encouraged in us ourselves a little of the nobility in which we were prepared to believe.

Index